INTRODUCTION

Welcome to the world of digital publishing ~ the book you now hold in your hand, while unchanged from the original **1959** edition, was printed using the latest state of the art digital technology. The advent of print-on-demand has forever changed the publishing process, never has information been so accessible and it is our hope that this book serves your informational needs for years to come. If this is your first exposure to digital publishing, we hope that you are pleased with the results. Many more titles of interest to the classic automobile and motorcycle enthusiast, collector and restorer are available via our website at **www.VelocePress.com.** We hope that you find this title as interesting as we do.

NOTE FROM THE PUBLISHER

The information presented is true and complete to the best of our knowledge. All recommendations are made without any guarantees on the part of the author or the publisher, who also disclaim all liability incurred with the use of this information.

TRADEMARKS

We recognize that some words, model names and designations, for example, mentioned herein are the property of the trademark holder. We use them for identification purposes only. This is not an official publication.

INFORMATION ON THE USE OF THIS PUBLICATION

This manual is an invaluable resource for the classic **VW** enthusiast and a "must have" for owners interested in increasing the performance of their vehicle. However, in today's information age we are constantly subject to changes in common practice, new technology, availability of improved materials and increased awareness of chemical toxicity. As such, it is advised that the user consult with an experienced professional prior to undertaking any procedure described herein. While every care has been taken to ensure correctness of information, it is obviously not possible to guarantee complete freedom from errors or omissions or to accept liability arising from such errors or omissions. Therefore, any individual that uses the information contained within, or elects to perform or participate in do-it-yourself repairs or modifications acknowledges that there is a risk factor involved and that the publisher or its associates cannot be held responsible for personal injury or property damage resulting from the use of the information or the outcome of such procedures.

While many of the manufacturers of the performance items referenced within may no longer be in business and prices have changed considerably since 1959, many new suppliers have come forward with alternate products aimed at increased performance. In addition, many of the vintage parts routinely turn up at swap meets and can also be obtained through a variety of vintage performance parts suppliers. Therefore, we hope that the information contained within helps in the identification of original vintage parts and provides the reader with appropriate data to aid in the selection of the newer performance products that are currently available.

It is important that the reader recognizes that any instructions may refer to either the right-hand or left-hand sides of the vehicle or the components and that the directions are followed carefully. One final word of advice, this publication is intended to be used as a reference guide, and when in doubt the reader should consult with a qualified technician.

SOUPING THE VOLKSWAGEN

by
DICK MORGAN

Copyrighted and Published 1959
FLOYD CLYMER PUBLICATIONS
World's Largest Publisher of Books Pertaining to
Automobiles, Motorcycles, Motor Racing and Americana
1268 South Alvarado Street
Los Angeles 6, California

ACKNOWLEDGEMENTS

Acknowledgements are hereby gratefully given for the invaluable help received from the following sources:

Advanced Car Specialties, Toronto, Canada.
Frank Atkinson, San Gabriel, California.
Beck Distributing Company, New York, New York.
California Sports Car, North Hollywood, California.
Car Technik, Toronto, Canada.
O. W. Dietz Engineering Company, Roseville, Michigan.
European Car Guide, New York, New York.
European Motor Products, Riverside, California.
Fisher Products, Long Island City, New York.
Iskenderian Cams, Inglewood, California.
Jahn's Quality Pistons, Los Angeles, California.
Judson Research and Manufacturing Company, Conshohocken, Pennsylvania.
McAfee Motors, Sherman Oaks, California.
Metal Improvement Company, Los Angeles, California.
Michelmore Motors, Reseda, California.
Louis B. Pierlot, Inglewood, California.
VDO Instruments, Detroit, Michigan.
Weber Tool Company, Los Angeles, California.

An Announcement

In presenting this new book SOUPING THE VOLKSWAGEN we are offering the first and most complete information ever published on speed tuning Volkswagen cars.

The Author, G. R. Morgan, is not only an engineer but is a practical man as well. He actually did the "souping" work on his own Volkswagen and assisted other Volkswagen owners in similar work. Therefore, his experience has been practical and not gained by a lot of theoretical ideas propounded by some one who has not had the actual experience that Mr. Morgan acquired.

We wish also to advise the reader that the Volkswagen Company has never been keen on speed tuning or "hopping up" their products. They feel that the car should be operated just as delivered to the customer. Americans, however, are a unique breed of individuals. Certainly thousands are going to do everything possible to increase the performance of their cars, whether it be a Volkswagen, Ford, Chevrolet, Plymouth or any other make. Americans are a bunch of amateur inventors, tinkerers, or call them what you will, who have an intense desire to find out what makes anything tick.

When we published our book on HOW TO HOP UP CHEVROLET ENGINES, at that time Chevrolet was not interested in speed tuning their products but there was a revolution going on in the United States regarding every phase of motoring. Now all U. S. makers have accepted the idea that their products are going to be altered in many different ways—in fact, many times the changes are so great that even their own engineers would hardly recognize what has been done by the amateur and the professional car enthusiasts in this country.

We are publishing this book because we feel that we should publish any book about any subject in which the car enthusiast in this country is interested. If we didn't publish this book somebody else would. With our reputation for publishing all types of automotive publications, we would have been foolish not to have accepted this book for publication when Mr. Morgan offered it to us.

Floyd Clymer

Publisher.

TABLE OF CONTENTS

Foreword		5
Introduction		7
Section One	WHY?	9
Section Two	PERFORMANCE	13
Section Three	FUNDAMENTALS OF POWER OUTPUT	16
Section Four	DESIGNING FOR HIGH POWER	23
Section Five	THE TOP END	28
Section Six	THE BOTTOM END	37
Section Seven	ASSEMBLY AND DISASSEMBLY	49
Section Eight	LUBRICATION	62
Section Nine	IGNITION	65
Section Ten	CLUTCH AND FLYWHEEL	67
Section Eleven	COOLING	69
Section Twelve	ENGINE PERFORMANCE	71
Section Thirteen	TUNE-UP INSTRUCTIONS	79
Section Fourteen	STATISTICS AND TECHNICAL DATA	82
Section Fifteen	CARBURETOR TROUBLE CHECKING	92
Section Sixteen	FUEL PUMP TROUBLE CHECKING	93
Section Seventeen	GENERATOR TROUBLE CHECKING	93
Section Eighteen	STARTING MOTOR TROUBLE CHECKING	94
Section Nineteen	CLUTCH TROUBLE CHECKING	95
Section Twenty	STEERING TROUBLE CHECKING	96
Section Twenty-one	BRAKE TROUBLE CHECKING	98
Section Twenty-two	DECIMAL EQUIVALENTS	99
Section Twenty-three	EXPLANATION OF ENGINE CAPACITY	99
Section Twenty-four	CHANGES BETWEEN VW MODELS	100
Section Twenty-five	SPARK PLUGS	102
Section Twenty-six	HINTS & TIPS by FLOYD CLYMER	103

All cartoons are by STAN MOTT. Mr. Mott's interesting and humorous cartoons have attracted national attention in motor magazines. He is doing an illustrated and humorous book for us that will be published soon. The title is "MAN MEETS VOLKSWAGEN." It's shock full of cartoons, humorous comments, anecdotes . . . a dozen laughs on every page. —Clymer.

INTRODUCTION

Retaliation and revenge at last for the long-suffering VW owners, who have had to put up with quaint jokes about the little old lady from Pasadena with a spare engine in her "trunk," or the one about the mainspring in the back.

If you have had my experience no amount of ducking down dark alleys, use of inadequate bath soaps, or insistence that you are not a VW owner have prevented you from hearing for the illionth time the one about the model airplane engine under the hood.

But all is not lost, for at last in this book we have the formula for success. After you have souped up your VW and wiped out all of the MG's and other small sedans at the neighborhood drag strip, the world takes on a different look. Now you can laugh when somebody tells a VW joke. The others will be laughing at the joke and you will be laughing at them.

Seriously, there are several good reasons, besides being a power psychopath, for souping a car like the VW. Most VW owners enjoy driving the car around town but find that it is lacking in *reserve power* on the open road. This is a common characteristic of almost all of the small imported economy sedans which have been designed for different driving and economic conditions than are found in the United States. Fortunately, however, in the factory efforts to keep the cost competitive and at rock bottom they have left considerable leeway for power increases in the engine.

This book outlines the work necessary to put the *reserve power* into your VW that leads to peace of mind and 100 percent relaxed driving under all conditions.

DICK MORGAN

ILLUSTRATIONS

Figure One	Relative fuel-to-air ratio	17
Figure Two	Volumetric efficiency of modern engine vs. VW breathing	18
Figure Three	Compression ratio terminology	21
Figure Four	BMEP Comparison, VW vs. Porsche	25
Figure Five	Dietz dual carb kit	29
Figure Six	Express dual carb kit	30
Figure Seven	Okrasa and stock VW heads	32
Figure Eight	Okrasa kit assembled	33
Figure Nine	Torque wrench and extender in use	51
Figure Ten	Use of wire to remove oil pressure valve	53
Figure Eleven	Checking clearance of flywheel on crankshaft	56
Figure Twelve	Shaft and rods prior to installation in crankcase	57
Figure Thirteen	Pierlot oil cooler	63
Figure Fourteen	EMPI clutch	68
Figure Fifteen	Power curves — stock bore & stroke	72
Figure Sixteen	Power curves with increased bore & stroke	74

TABLES

Table I	Comparison of modified VW's & other foreign cars	12
Table II	Valve port sizes required for maximum output	31
Table III	Comparison of types of camshafts	34
Table IV	Muffler back pressure	35
Table V	Distributor advance	65
Table VI	Fan belts	70
Table VII	Carburetor jets, a summary	80
Table VIII	Specification data	82
Table IX	Volkswagen weight data	83
Table X	Power/speed curves of various VW models	86
Table XI	Speed/rpm comparison for each gear	87

SECTION ONE

WHY?

Whenever the subject of hopping up cars is brought up in social circles a little flurry is always created. Some person who seems to be disgustingly logical (about other people's hobbies, not his own, of course) brings up the question:—"Why?"

The enthusiast is likely to be pinned to the wall if he does not have the correct answers. In fact, many times the enthusiast's own mind may prompt this question without a satisfactory answer.

To many of us, automobiles are a hobby, and thus it is difficult to justify the expense to a non-enthusiast. Oddly enough in this country which produces more automobiles than the rest of the world put together the automobile hobbyist does not enjoy a very high reputation. The average "man on the street" catalogs the automobile enthusiast in about the same category as butterfly collectors, poets, and tax collectors. He's a man who is tolerated but must constantly be watched lest he try to take over the country.

To those of us who are enthusiasts, no selling is needed on hopping up engines. Just the urge to obtain the finest performance possible is enough to spur us on. When the factory detunes an engine for man-in-the-street use it is like waving a red flag in front of the enthusiast.

However, since the advent of the small European economy sedan in this country there are good sound reasons for modifying for more power.

Around town most small economy sedans are really in their element. Top driving speed in congested areas is usually well under 50 miles per hour. Even freeway and through-way travel can be pleasant because little acceleration is required when passing cars as all cars are moving at about the same speed.

Out on the open road things are a little different. Have you ever tried to pass a car on a two-lane road doing about 60 miles per hour with a car that has a top speed of 70 miles per hour? You wait and wait until you can see about two miles straight ahead with no cars coming the other way. Then you swing out and about half way past the road takes a very slight imperceptible up-turn and your top speed is now reduced to 65 miles per hour. Your passing acceleration is now cut in half and you begin to sweat a little. The guy you are passing sees that you have one of those "funny little cars" and speeds up a couple of miles per hour to get a "good long look."

WHY?

You are now three-fourths of the way past him and a fast car appears over the horizon heading toward you. Now the sweat really begins to roll. Is the guy beside you going to ease up just a trifle and let you squeak in, or are you entirely on your own to make it? Or should you back off and try again later? You can't stop now as you have been following him for ten miles waiting for this chance.

Tune in next week and see if he made it. Guaranteed to cure any over-weight problem. Carry a spare accelerator pedal with you, the old one will become bent and broken during a long trip. If you are squeamish don't read the next paragraph.

You are driving from Los Angeles to Las Vegas. Everything goes very smoothly until you hit the desert. The *BIG* desert, past Baker, California. What is wrong? Your foot is to the floor-board but you cannot go faster than 45 miles per hour. You are on a twenty-mile-long up-grade, straight as an arrow, with a 15 mph head-wind. You jockey the gearshift back and forth between third and fourth, but very little happens. Beside, you're red-lined in third at 48 miles per hour. It seems as though you could walk this fast, but finally you get used to it. You don't realize how slow you are going until cars doing 65 or 70 start passing you. A little traffic is coming the other way now and you are getting slightly embarrassed because cars are starting to stack up behind and you are muttering under your breath because you can't do a thing about it. You now come up behind a big diesel rig doing about 35 under these conditions. Traffic coming against you is a long way off but you have had to slow down slightly behind the truck. Should you pull out right away and risk it? It takes 15 seconds to pass a large truck with your speed but all of the other cars behind you are closing in and expecting to pass with you. It will only take them about five seconds and they expect the same of you. However, half-way around with everyone behind you, you now observe that the lead car coming down the hill toward you is another small economy sedan driver doing about 80 miles per hour to make up for *his* 40 mile per hour stint coming up the other side. Ball of snakes, anyone?

Don't let us scare you away from buying a small car, for nothing is as much fun, nor as easy to wheel around in as a car weighing between 1500 and 2500 pounds. But to enjoy completely relaxed driving under all conditions in this country a certain minimum power-to-weight ratio is needed to give adequate *reserve power*. Only one of two small sedans sold in this country come anywhere near meeting this requirement. Fortunately, most of the sedans can be souped up to meet the requirement and will give economical and reliable service for many years.

WHY?

Owners of the Volkswagen are fortunate because there is more power to be obtained from their engine than from many other imports. The light weight provides for astounding acceleration. Although the top speed can be increased it is only a result of the *reserve power* built in to give you peace of mind regardless of traffic and road conditions.

We cannot do anything to improve the aerodynamics of the body which make it unsafe to drive at speeds above 75 miles per hour.

Many people will be shocked of course that we recommend up to 100 per cent increases in power without improving brakes and handling. If you were to increase your top driving speed, of course handling and brakes must be improved accordingly. The VW cannot be driven safely regardless of brakes or handling at speeds above which people are now driving them. Even the VW factory which is quite conservative allows cruising speeds equal to the top speed of the car, that is, 70 to 75 miles per hour.

The next subject of interest is the economy angle. Why not just buy a larger more powerful car or a sports car?

Sports cars come in small sizes too, but if you or your family have definitely decided that you need more space than most sports cars have, then you are back to small economy sedans for good handling.

Larger cars are more powerful but of course can cost quite a chunk of dough. Hopping up small cars can still be considerably cheaper than buying a large car. Also, small cars can always be detuned to stock condition and will usually bring a good price as transportation cars when they're old and tired.

The accompanying Table compares the price of a souped up Volkswagen with the basic list price of other small sedans and sports cars of comparable performance. In the instance of the VW, including the Karmann-Ghia, $500 has been added to the basic list to give a comparison. It can readily be seen that the prices (for a VW *with* the additional expenditure for souping-up) are *still* reasonable. Other advantages such as longer tire life, cheaper service, and high resale, are in no way minimized.

WHY?

MODEL	BASIC LIST PRICE (P.O.E. East Coast, without accessories, sales tax or license)	0-60 mph in seconds
VW sedan, de luxe	$2045 ($1545 + 500)	15
VW Karmann-Ghia	$2900 ($2400 + 500)	15
Volvo PV 444	$2340	15
MG A	$2460	14
Porsche 1600 coupe	$3660	14

TABLE I
Comparison of modified VW with cars of similar performance.

SECTION TWO
PERFORMANCE

The ultimate objective, of course, is the performance that you can expect with a certain modification. Here again it is impossible to build and test all of the possible modifications, but some general ground rules will be established so that you can estimate your performance if you know the engine power output.

Before we proceed any further, let's get it straight that the only performance that we are going to discuss will be acceleration and hill-climbing ability. High speeds are not for the VW sedan and transporter. Theoretically Karmann-Ghia folk can drive faster safely since they enjoy the advantages of better aerodynamics. However, sustained high speed driving will seriously tax the brakes of all VW's because they are not designed for it.

If you really are a high speed nut then you must buy a car that is designed for high speed. Such things as braking power, braking directional stability, aerodynamic directional stability, susceptibility to gusts and side winds are all factors that must be considered at high speed. The VW particularly is deficient in all of these departments and just cannot be driven consistently safely at speeds over 70 mph.

Actually it is difficult these days to drive very far over 70 mph except on race tracks. Keeping in mind traffic density, road conditions, and law enforcement it is wise not to exceed this speed except on rare occasions.

What we are trying to build into the VW mainspring compartment is enough *reserve power* so that you can relax and enjoy driving when encountering the usual obstacles of hills, headwinds, and slower cars. If all roads were level, and without other cars, then the power of the typical European economy sedan would be adequate and everybody would be happy.

However, it is well known by now that one of the most common complaints of the owners of small economy sedans, in this country, is lack of power.

How much power do you need for relaxed driving? Naturally, everyone's tastes vary, but a good minimum is probably represented by the most popular low-priced American cars built between 1946 and 1952, before the horsepower race began. No one complained about a lack of power in these cars, and performance, for the most part, was satisfactory.

PERFORMANCE

The ratio of car weight to engine power is a good indicator of car performance. The typical low priced car of this period weighed about 3500 pounds with two people and put out about 110 hp, giving a power-to-weight ratio of 32 pounds per horsepower. Higher values mean that the performance is poorer and lower values mean better performance.

With two people a Volkswagen sedan weighs in at 2000 pounds. The weight-to-power ratio is 56 lb./hp. If we are seeking the magic figure of 32 lb./hp then we must divide 2,000 by 32, giving 63 hp.

Even during the best years of the horsepower race 25 to 30 percent of all American cars sold were "economy" sixes with weight-to-power ratios no better than 27 lb./hp. It is presumed that the owners of these cars were satisfied with the performance or they would have purchased the more powerful V-8's.

In terms of actual performance the weight-to-power ratio has been found to be a very good indicator of acceleration and hill climbing ability. An analysis of the acceleration times from zero to 60 indicates that for a large number of cars the time in seconds is equal to one-half of the pounds of test weight per rated horsepower.

Applying this to the VW with 56 lb./hp computed 0 to 60 time is 28 seconds. Road tests generally turn in 28 to 30 seconds.

The Volvo 85 hp PV444 figures 14.7 seconds with an actual 14.3.

MG A is about two seconds off with a calculated value of 16 and a true value of 14 seconds.

The Porsche 1500 coupe calculates to 17 with a true of 15 seconds. Even this amount of agreement is remarkable when considering vagaries of different factory engine ratings, climate, driving techniques, and automobile condition. The method is accurate enough to give a good indication within a second or two what we can do with the VW.

How much power will we need to stay with an MG A or Porsche 1500 coupe? Consulting the formula and assuming a total car weight of 2000 lbs., 60 horsepower will give a weight-to-power ratio of 30, with a resultant 15 seconds 0-to-60 time.

If we go way out and soup up to the maximum potential of 90 hp, weight-to-power will be 22, with a 0 to 60 time of 11 seconds. Since the weight-to-power ratiowillbe 15 per cent better than the 1500 Porsche Super and a good 10 per cent better than the 1600 Super, little trouble should be experienced beating these cars up to 60 mph. Beyond this speed of course the drag of the VW sedan is much higher. The lower drag of the K-G coupe should cope with the Porsche for a higher range but VW fourth gear does not correctly match engine and car power for maximum top speed.

PERFORMANCE

With a moderate weight-to-power ratio, 30 lb./hp, you will be able to retain a cruising speed of 65 to 70 mph on most long straight grades but you may have to use third gear. One of the advantages of having a high-speed, free-breathing engine in the VW is that car speeds may go up to 65-70 in third making it a nice choice for high speed passing and hill climbing. This is a tremendous improvement over the stock engine which is very exasperating, having a limit on third around 50 mph. Many times you either have to shift, or run out of breath, just when you are passing another car.

This section would not be complete without a word or two about performance of theTransporter series of VW vehicles.

TheTransporter,Micro bus, andKombi all weigh about 800 pounds more than the sedan and naturally suffer in the performance department. Top speed in stock form is usually close to 60 mph so that 0-to-60 times are difficult if not impossible to record.

Relative performance increases should be the same for the bus as the sedan but at a correspondingly slower speed. Thus if the engine power is doubled, 0-to-50 times should be cut about in half and top speed should reach close to the 70 mph mark. Hills may be taken at 50 to 55 in third, as against 35 to 40 mph prior to modification.

Well, we have just about red-lined ourselves in this section and we will shift to the next cog for some fundamentals of power output.

Stan Mott

How Cape Canaveral employees would speed tune a Volkswagen.

SECTION THREE

FUNDAMENTALS OF POWER OUTPUT

We will try not to go too hot and heavy into the fundamentals of power output of internal combustion engines, but a little background makes it a lot easier in the work to follow.

The power output of almost any internal combustion engine whether it be reciprocating (automobile type) or gas turbine (turbojet and turboprop engines) depends primarily on the following three factors:

1. The weight flow of combustion gases that can be "pumped" through the engine per minute.
2. The amount of energy released during the combustion process.
3. The *expansion ratio* of the combustion gases.

There are other secondary factors such as friction of the moving parts and heat losses through the cooling fluid. We do what we can to keep power losses from these areas down to a minimum but our main concentration will be to *up* the power obtained from the main contributing factors. We will take the three main sources of power output itemized above and go into them in more detail.

WEIGHT FLOW OF COMBUSTION GASES

Increasing the weight flow of the combustion gases through the engine is the most fruitful source of power increases.

What the cylinders draw in, on the intake stroke, later to be burned, is a mixture of fuel (gasoline, alcohol, or what have you) and air. During the combustion period of the cycle the mixture burns or ignites. The hot combustion gases then expand and thus "push" on the piston during the power stroke, resulting in the "go" we are all familiar with. The important thing to remember is that the more fuel-air mixture that we can get into cylinders, the more "push" that will be exerted on the piston, resulting in more power output.

Since we now know that we need as much fuel-air mixture in the cylinders as we can possibly get, the next natural question arises as to the proper ratio of fuel to air to obtain maximum power from the engine. Both theory and practice are very much in agreement, with the result that maximum power is released when approximately 16 pounds of air are burned with every pound of fuel, when using gasoline.

FUNDAMENTALS OF POWER OUTPUT

One of the important jobs of the carburetor on your car is the adjustment of the fuel flow so the mixture does not vary appreciably from this sixteen-to-one ratio under widely varying conditions of engine speed and throttle position. During part-throttle driving, when maximum economy is desired, the mixture ratio becomes slightly leaner. Maximum power is achieved at slightly richer (more fuel) mixture ratios.

Since air is much lighter than gasoline and we need sixteen times as much air by *weight* as gasoline, we begin to understand why the air passages in a carburetor are so much larger than the fuel passages.

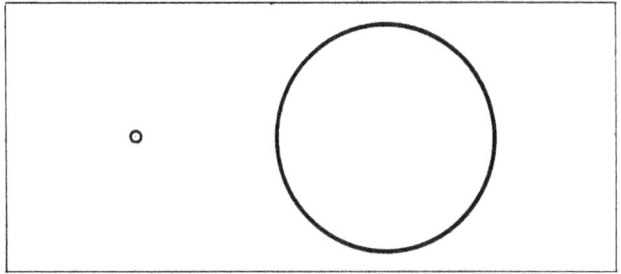

FIGURE 1. *Relative space occupied by fuel (left) and air (right) when mixed in the proper 16 to 1 ratio.*

Figure 1 shows the relative space occupied by the fuel and air in the proper mixture ratio. It will be immediately observed by those who have worked on engines that these are approximately the relative sizes of the air and fuel passages in a normal carburetor.

It does little good to increase the fuel flow to an engine unless a corresponding increase in air flow can be achieved at the same time. Since the engine porting for air is much larger than that required for fuel it is obvious where the problems lie.

There are two fundamental ways of increasing the air flow in an engine. The first and most obvious way is to force more air in under positive pressure, as with supercharging. In the absence of supercharging, the second method reduces the resistance to the air flow by increasing the air passages by means of larger valves, shorter manifolds, or individual manifolds and carburetors for each cylinder, and induction tuning. In the unsupercharged engine the measure of how well the job has been done is referred to as "volumetric efficiency". Volumetric efficiency is the ratio of the actual pounds of air that is packed into a cylinder to a theoretical amount were there no restrictions whatsoever in the induction passages.

FUNDAMENTALS OF POWER OUTPUT

Figure 2 shows the volumetric efficiency of a modern engine, together with the estimated efficiency of the "breathing" of a VW engine for comparison.

We have to estimate the VW curve since it takes large and expensive equipment to make these measurements, which we do not have at our disposal.

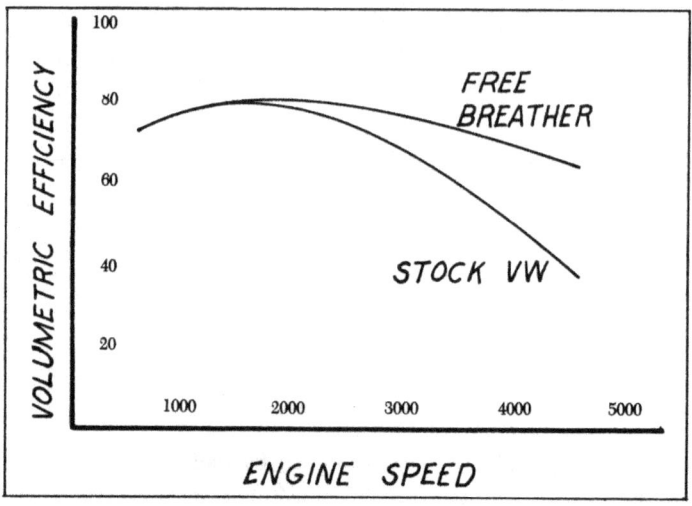

FIGURE 2. This chart shows that with increased engine speed, the stock Volkswagen engine, due to "poor breathing," is lacking in volumetric efficiency compared with an engine modified to give better passage of gases in and out.

It can be seen that the VW is satisfactory for the low revolutions for which the engine was originally intended, but the curve takes a nose-dive at the high rpm end where the greatest power is obtained.

Because power is a measure of the ultimate work ability of the engine and depends on the amount of air we can push through per minute it is obvious that high power depends on high rpm's. If volumetric efficiency did not change, 6000 rpm would give us twice as much power as 3000 rpm. The main limiting factors of today's high speed engines are the strength of the crank, connecting rods, and bearings to withstand high speeds, and the problem of valve float.

The VW engine has been especially choked down with small valves, single carburetor, and small exhausts to give exceptionally long life. It has ben well established that the VW engine has two to four times the life of other small economy cars because of this

FUNDAMENTALS OF POWER OUTPUT

detuning. For this reason when the engine is opened up and allowed to breathe freely as other modern engines do, worlds of power is available with only a small loss of life and reliability.

ENERGY RELEASED DURING COMBUSTION PROCESS

The energy released during the combustion process is not very sensitive to the engine design and is approximately 18,000 BTU's per pound of gasoline when burned with air in the 16 to 1 ratio mentioned previously.

Combustion chamber shape is not an important factor in energy release but it does determine the maximum compression ratio at which the fuel may be burned. Higher compression ratios do not release more energy but they do allow the gases to be compressed to higher pressures, which means more power during the expansion stroke.

The heat energy released during the combustion process heats the combustion gases to 3000 to 3500 degrees F. during part of the stroke when the combustion chamber volume, formed by the top of the piston and the cylinder head, is approximately constant size. Since the gases are restricted to this fixed volume the pressure must rise enormously due to heating, and this pressure is what does the work during the power stroke.

Detonation is the limiting factor determining the highest pressures that can occur in the combustion chamber before ignition. Detonation can be controlled somewhat by combustion chamber shape, and the type of combustion chamber that seems to control detonation most efficiently is the wedge type now found on most American V8 engines.

Fuel octane rating is also very important and the higher the octane rating the more the mixture can be compressed before detonation occurs. Detonation is to be avoided like the plague because it means loss of power, overheating, and extreme hammer-like blows to the pistons and connecting rods. Wild pressure surges do no useful work on the piston, and in large doses can cause an engine to fail in short order.

One more thing that is very important, of course, is the spark necessary to ignite the fuel-air mixture. A certain minimum spark size is necessary to ignite the mixture properly. Beyond this requirement very little power is gained by using bigger, fatter, or multiple spark sources. For high speed racing engines the extra power gained, better combustion control, and extra reliability warrant dual ignition systems.

FUNDAMENTALS OF POWER OUTPUT

Higher pressures due to high compression ratios may require a hotter coil. Check this the next time you have your spark plugs cleaned and tested. The plugs are usually inserted in a pressurized chamber and subjected to a continuous spark. The spark gets weaker with increasing pressure until the plug no longer fires. This is the reason that high compression ratios need a hotter spark. The spark, of course, must be timed at just the right instant to give maximum power, and this timing varies considerably with engine speed and cylinder pressure. The distributor automatically compensates for these two different effects in two different ways.

Every distributor contains a centrifugal advance mechanism which adjusts the spark to fire earlier during the piston stroke as engine speed goes up. This is because the combustion process takes a fixed amount of time and must be started earlier at high speeds, so that the burning will be complete when the piston starts down on the power stroke.

Most modern distributors have a vacuum advance that adjusts the spark to fire earlier under part throttle when the inlet manifold has a high vacuum. This improves the gasoline mileage by assuring complete combustion under low pressure. During wide-open throttle operation the vacuum mechanism retards the spark to a setting determined by the centrifugal advance for maximum power.

When modifying an engine for extra power output the spark advance curve usually changes, but it is not always possible to reset the distributor for maximum power over the complete speed range.

If enough demand exists for distributors for a particular make of engine, some manufacturer usually produces a high quality unit.

EXPANSION OR POWER STROKE

Those of you familiar with piston engines have probably learned by now that the power stroke is the time at which the hot combustion gases work on the piston. This is the real payoff point. All the other processes such as intake, compression, combustion, and exhaust exist only so that during the power stroke the high pressure gases can exert maximum "push" on the piston and convert thermodynamic energy into mechanical energy.

Although much talk is heard about the compression ratio of an engine it is really the expansion ratio that determines how efficiently the high pressure gases convert their pressure energy into mechanical energy.

FUNDAMENTALS OF POWER OUTPUT

The expansion ratio (or compression ratio) is defined as relation of the total cylinder volume when the piston is at the extreme bottom of its travel to the volume when it is at the very top of its stroke. Figure 3 illustrates this. Note that the compression ratio is computed by adding the piston or engine displacement volume to the clearance volume in order to obtain the total volume when the piston is down. Also note that the clearance volume when the piston is all of the way up not only includes the head volume but may contain some volume that is left in the cylinder.

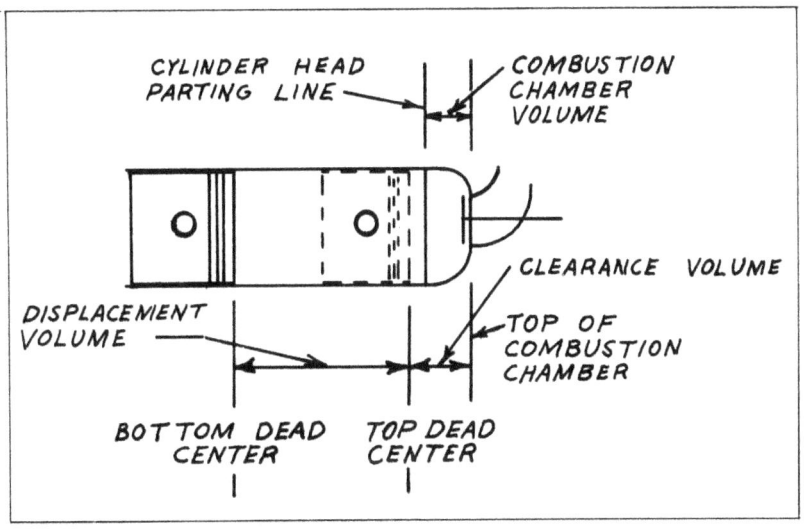

FIGURE 3. Study of this drawing will show the significance of terminology employed in discussion of compression ratio and similar points. The middle cylinder has piston to the left, but a phantom piston to the right in order to show the difference between bottom and top dead centers.

Higher expansion ratios allow the gases to expand to a lower pressure before they are exhausted, thus extracting more energy.

The effect of compression ratio is presented thus: If R is the compression ratio the curve follows this formula:

$$\frac{R^{.4}-1}{R^{.4}}$$

We have discussed the fundamentals in obtaining power out of a piston engine and hope that you have made some sense out of it. Let's put all of these different things together and see just what kind of an engine will give us maximum power.

FUNDAMENTALS OF POWER OUTPUT

Power is the time-rate of doing work or energy conversion. To get the most power out of an engine we must cram a maximum mixture of gas and air through the engine per minute. If it were not for limitations imposed by stresses on rotating and reciprocating parts, and if a drop-off in volumetric efficiency at high speeds could be prevented, there is no reason why engines could not be run at 10,000, 20,000, or even 30,000 rpm to obtain fantastic power outputs.

We have to live with these mechanical limitations, however, and the best designed engine is one where all of the limitations show up simultaneously at the maximum top speed. In pursuing this ideal, modern high-speed engines are designed with big bore, short stroke, and large valves. Most high output engines have bore-to-stroke ratios of 1.0 to 1.3 with extremely large valves and intake passages.

Stan Mott

The Civil War veteran enthusiast's idea of souping the Volkswagen.

SECTION FOUR
DESIGNING FOR HIGH POWER

We have to talk about one thing at a time and the most natural dividing line is the top of the piston. Visualize an engine with the pistons moving in a vertical direction above the crankshaft—such as an MG. Everything above the top of the piston including the intake manifold, valves, carburetors and exhaust is called the "top end". Everything below the top of the piston such as connecting rods, crankshaft, rod bearings, main bearings, and the piston itself is called the "bottom end". There are lots of different layouts where the so-called top end is on the bottom, the bottom end may be on the side, etc., but we still use these terms because everyone understands what they mean.

The top end is primarily concerned with generating the gases that do all of the work. The bottom end's job is to see that the heat energy is converted to mechanical rotational energy. For maximum power it's the top end's job to see that maximum weight of air-fuel mixture goes through and is burned the most efficient way possible, while the bottom end has to hold together under the stresses of high reciprocating and rotating speeds. The camshaft is usually located in the bottom end, but controls the valve timing so that it is considered part of the top end.

The VW engine is a "pancake" type with the top end(s) on the sides, and the bottom end in the center, but we'll stick to conventional terms.

The VW engine that Dr. Porsche designed 25 years ago has many features that are up-to-date such as short stroke, low weight, and overhead valve design. Although the engine enjoys these basic features the fact that it was originally conceived as an economy car, and has changed very little since, leaves much room for improvement where maximum power is concerned. The very fact that Dr. Porsche himself souped up the VW engine for use in the Porsche automobile speaks for the soundness of the basic design. The Porsche Super engine of 70 horsepower puts out almost three times the power of the 25 horsepower VW using the VW crankcase with only slight modifications.

A fundamental unit that tells us how efficient the engine is as far as power output is concerned, regardless of size, is BMEP or Brake Mean Effective Pressure. BMEP is the theoretical pressure that would have to be exerted continuously during the power stroke of an engine to give the necessary power output. It is obviously

DESIGNING FOR HIGH POWER

not an actual pressure since the gas pressure during the power stroke varies over a wide range. BMEP does have definite merit in comparing engine performance. It lumps volumetric efficiency, cam timing, combustion, and crank angle all into one neat package that gives a sound basis for comparison regardless of engine size or speed.

BMEP is related to power output by the following equation:

$$BHP = \frac{BMEP \times A \times N \times S}{66,000}$$

where:
BHP = Brake horsepower (generated at the flywheel)
BMEP = Brake Mean Effective Pressure in psi
A = Total piston area in square inches
N = Speed in revolutions per minute
S = Stroke in feet

BMEP is computed by measuring the actual power output of an engine with a water brake or eddy current dynamometer. The only other factors needed are the engine dimensions which can be readily measured. When computing the BMEP the above equation of course has to be turned around thus:

$$BMEP = \frac{66,000 \times BHP}{A \times N \times S}$$

As an example let's take the stock VW engine and compute its BMEP. By comparing this with other engines we can see whether we are behind or ahead of the times as far as the power output is concerned. We will consider the 36 horsepower model, as it is the latest. SAE horsepower rating is used since it will be most comparable with other cars.

BHP = 36
N = 3700 rpm
Vol = 72.7 cubic inches

$$BMEP = \frac{792,000 \times 36}{3700 \times 72.7}$$

BMEP = 106 psi

BMEP depends on volumetric efficiency and other factors that in turn depend on engine speed. Figure 4 shows the BMEP of the VW compared with a typical high performance sports car engine of similar size and construction, the Porsche. Notice that the peak BMEP of the Porsche engine is only slightly higher than the VW but that it does not drop off as rapidly at high speed.

DESIGNING FOR HIGH POWER

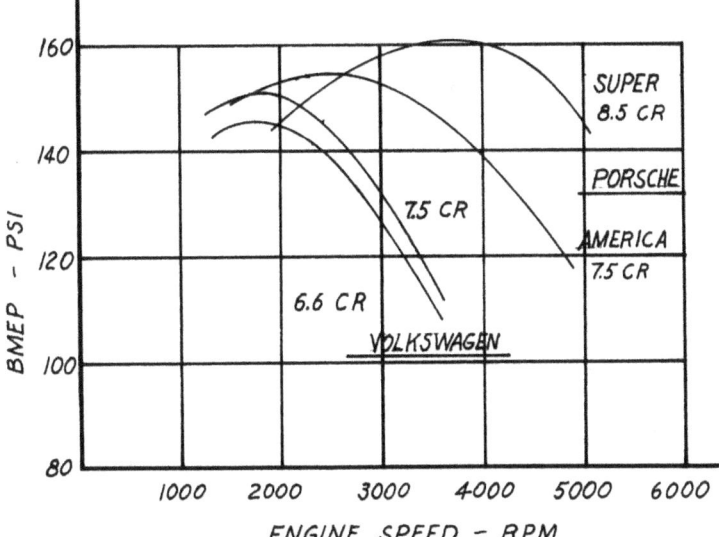

FIGURE 4. Comparison of Brake Mean Effective Pressure of VW and Porsche.

The BMEP is a measure of how much air is packed into the cylinder and the expansion ratio (compression ratio) of the combustion gases. At low engine speed with low velocity air in the induction system, the small valves and carburetion of the VW present little restriction and the cylinders are filled just as well as any engine. When the engine tries to draw in a higher flow of air at high engine speed the choking effect of the small induction system offsets this effort.

Since power is the product of BMEP and engine speed, N, we can see the rewards of keeping the BMEP as high as possible in the high rpm range. This is accomplished by using large ports, carburetors, and valves to reduce restrictions to the incoming air, thus obtaining maximum cylinder filling.

Another improvement that can be made is to shift the BMEP curve to the right, gaining more power at the high end and losing power at the low end. This is accomplished by timing the valves to allow for inertia lag of the gases, thus filling the cylinders better at high speed. Cams that are ground to favor high speed operation are called "full race," "sports," "¾ race," "track," "competition," etc. These all have varying degrees of timing depending upon how much smoothness and flexibility can be sacrificed at low engine speed.

DESIGNING FOR HIGH POWER

A considerable improvement in power over stock cams, retaining relatively good idle and low speed flexibility, can be obtained by stopping just short of the full race grind.

We have mentioned the limitations of the induction system—they can be grouped in two categories:

1. Friction and pressure losses in the intake manifold and carburetors due to high velocity gases.

2. Inertia lag of the gases entering and leaving the cylinder.

The first effect is due to inherent friction between the walls of the manifold and the gases, as well as restriction such as valves and carburetor parts. Wall friction can be minimized by using large, short-length manifolds, eliminating as many bends as possible, and smoothing the interior passages. As the carburetor itself acts as a restriction, using the maximum size carburetor is important. Overhead valve engines, with passages to the combustion chamber straight and direct provide the least restriction.

The second effect due to inertia of the incoming mixture and exhaust gases is a little difficult to explain, but may be illustrated this way:—when the piston is going down on the intake stroke, the intake valve is open and the mixture is being drawn into the cylinders by suction. At low speed the mixture follows the movement of the piston precisely. As soon as the intake valve opens the mixture enters the cylinder, and as soon as the intake valve closes the mixture is cut off. In reality it takes a small but finite time for the gases to start moving when the intake valve opens, but this is not noticed at low speed because the time involved is very short compared to the time of piston travel.

At high speed, however, the time required to start and stop the mixture is large compared with the time of piston travel and the gases don't really flow into the cylinders at a decent rate before the intake valve closes. The same thing happens during the exhaust stroke when the gases have to be "pushed" out of the cylinder to make way for the new charge. The answer to the proper filling of the cylinder lies in the valve timing, controlled by the camshaft. High speed cams open the valves a little earlier, and close them a little later, for maximum cylinder "filling" of the combustible fuel mixture.

Engines that are designed to run at low speed have camshafts that control the timing so that the valves open and close near the top dead center and bottom dead center of the piston travel, as indicated by engine theory when gas inertia effects are minimal.

DESIGNING FOR HIGH POWER

However, high speed engines, from which maximum power is derived, have camshafts that allow for the inertia effect, and open the valves *sooner*, and close them *later*, than indicated by simple engine theory.

Naturally, each type of engine is most efficient in the speed range for which it was designed.

Designing or modifying the VW for high power output requires better breathing at the top end, and an improved crankshaft at the bottom end. Economy of operation will not suffer if the extra power is used sparingly, only when it is really needed.

Stan Mott

The "beatniks" prefer the gas generator to save fuel.

SECTION FIVE

THE TOP END

The top is where all of the power is generated and will naturally receive the most attention. This section will discuss requirements for each improvement, and kits that are available.

CARBURETION AND INTAKE MANIFOLD

One of the chief disadvantages of the flat or pancake engine is the long and tortuous path of the induction manifold when using only one carburetor. Naturally we could not expect two carburetors to be used in a small, cheap, economy sedan. By switching to dual carburetors manifolding can be improved at the same time. Several dual carburetor kits are available on the market and can be installed quite easily without engine removal.

DIETZ DUAL CARBURETORS

The O. W. Dietz Engineering Company in Michigan produces a very complete dual carb kit designed to use the stock 28 PCI VW carbs. The following items are included for $48.00:

Polished aluminum dual intake manifold with equalizer tube.
Sturdy throttle linkage with adjustable tension.
Choke connection to one carb.
Gas lines with adapter to 6mm, VW system.
Heat riser cover plates.
Installation manual.

In addition an extra carburetor and air cleaner must be purchased for about $33.00 for a total outlay of $81.00.

The power curve furnished by Dietz comparing their kit with the stock VW engine indicates that gross power goes up from 36 to 42.5 for an increase of 18 per cent.

Installation can be accomplished without removing the engine. Remove the fan housing and generator as indicated in the manual. Remove stock intake manifold and install Dietz dual carbs as per instructions.

Figure 5 is a picture of the installation in a sedan.

THE TOP END

FIGURE 5. The Volkswagen engine breathing can be vastly improved through use of this Dietz dual carburetor kit, made in the USA.

EXPRESS DUAL CARBURETORS

Car Technik in Toronto, Canada, is importing a German-made dual carb kit that has been in use in Germany for over five years and is endorsed by the German Auto Club. It is designed to use the stock 28 PCI carbs and sells complete for $117.00. The following items are included:

28 PCI carburetor.
Conversion kit for present carburetor.
Dual intake manifolds.
Heat risers.
Oil bath air cleaners.
Equalizer tube.
All throttle linkage and gas lines.

The kit is complete, with no other purchases necessary, but is slightly more expensive than the Dietz kit. However, it does retain the heat riser tubes which can be an advantage if you do much starting in cold weather. The heat risers prevent ice from forming in the intake manifold while the engine is warming up, and can prevent frequent stalling during this period of driving.

Car Technik claims a 25 per cent power increase but dynamometer data are not available for exact comparison with Dietz. Since the same carburetors are used in both kits, together with similar intake manifolds, it is reasonable that power and performance increases are within a few per cent of each other.

THE TOP END

FIGURE 6. The "Express" dual carburetor kit for Volkswagen is made in Germany.

Figure 6 shows installation of the Express kit. The kit may be installed by removing the fan and generator as per instructions in the VW manual.

VALVES AND PORTING

The biggest stumbling block in souping the VW is the size of the valves and valve ports. Table II provided by Ed Iskenderian shows the sizes of intake and exhaust ports needed for internal combustion engines dependent upon speed and engine size. Checking the stock Volks running at a peak speed of 3700 rpm we see that the intake and exhaust port size needed are 1.0 and .85 inches respectively.

Engines built after January 1954 are well designed for this speed as they have intake and exhaust ports of 1.00 and .95 inches respectively. This shows that the VW is well-designed for its intended purpose. However, as our sights are on the 5000 to 5500 rpm range we can see from the chart that minimum port sizes of 1.20 and 1.01 inches are needed for intake and exhaust. The stock exhaust ports come pretty close, but the intakes fall far short.

An even worse problem is the induction passage in the head, feeding the valve ports. The passage connecting to the intake manifold is the size of one valve port but must feed *two* cylinders. This is called "siamese porting" and although practiced extensively on production automobiles, is generally recognized as a poor arrangement for maximum power output.

THE TOP END

Displacement		Intake		Exhaust	
cc.	cu. in.	mm.	in.	mm.	in.
1192	72.7	30.5	1.20	25.5	1.01
1300	79.2	32	1.25	26.5	1.05
1500	91.5	34	1.33	28.5	1.13

TABLE II
Valve port sizes needed for maximum output at 5,000 rpm.

Larger valves can be installed in the stock VW head and the ports can be enlarged, but the whole operation is rather tricky. Very little extra metal has been left to grind out and it is difficult to get into the remote passages.

OKRASA

The best and by far the easiest way to improve the situation is to buy new heads that already incorporate all the necessary changes. The Okrasa Company in West Germany has been making such a head kit for several years.

The Okrasa exhaust valves and passages are stock VW but the intake system is considerably larger. Intake valves are 1.30 inches compared to the stock 1.18 inches, and the intake ports are 1.10 inches compared to .99 inches stock. Better still, the intake ports are not siamesed and each cylinder is fed by its own port larger than the single port of the stocker which feeds two cylinders.

The Okrasa head kit is imported from Germany by European Motor Products Company in California. It is popular both here and in Germany for obtaining a fat power increase. The kit is very complete and sells for $250. This is reasonable if you consider that the Porsche carburetors that come with the kit alone sell for $43 each. With stock bore and stroke the kit is available in either 7.5 to 1 or 8.5 to 1 compression ratio. The following items are included:

    2 special heads with large valves and ports.
    2 intake manifolds.
    2 Porsche 32mm PBI carburetors.
    2 special air cleaners.
    Throttle linkage, fuel lines, and all bolts and washers.
    Instructions.

The kit does not take much time to install.

Figure 7 shows the comparison of the Okrasa head in intake porting with a stock VW head.

THE TOP END

FIGURE 7. Extra port area which will improve the Volkswagen engine's "breathing" is shown in these Okrasa cylinder heads.

Figure 8 shows the kit completely assembled (without engine). A 33 per cent increase in power is obtainable using the Okrasa head kit, with no other basic changes. Approximately 4 per cent of this is due to increase in compression ratio, leaving 29 per cent due to better breathing alone.

OKRASA MODIFIED

Even the Okrasa suffers somewhat if we head for the 5000 to 5500 rpm range but larger valves and heftier valve springs can be installed. Jaguar XK exhaust valves make sturdy intake valves as they have almost the exact dimensions needed. Jaguar double springs and retainers ca be used with little modification. New and larger seat inserts have to be shrunk into the head.

All of the latter work described above is of course for those who have access to machine shops, as end milling, boring and turning are all required. However, the results are worth it if you enjoy the ultimate in snappy performance and are handy with tools and machinery.

THE TOP END

FIGURE 8. *This gives a clear idea of the complete Okrasa dual carburetor head kit, as the view is not obscured by generator, cylinders and other components of the final assembly.*

VALVE TIMING (Camshaft)

Revised valve timing on the VW is a fruitful road to more power as the stock cam has an extremely low speed grind. Fortunately there is enough meat on the VW camshaft to change the valve timing and increase the valve lift at the same time. Iskenderian, Harman-Collins, and Weber are the big name cam grinders in this country who can probably furnish you any type of cam that you desire. Iskenderian was the first to regrind VW cams in this country and has about the largest selection. Except for racing, the Iskenderian 2B and 2J grinds take care of most road work. Both cams increase the valve timing to the same degree of opening and closing as the Porsche Super but the 2J cam has a more radical lift rate, which gives a long open time.

Both these cams have a good idle with no coughing or wheezing at low speed. Table III compares the pertinent specifications of the different cams.

THE TOP END

Cam	Intake opens BTDC	Intake closes ABDC	Exhaust opens BBDC	Exhaust closes ATDC	Type	Lift
VW stock	2.5°	37.5°	37.5°	2.5°	Stk	
2B	19	55	54	20	1/2	.318
2J	18	55	53	20	3/4	.335
Porsche Am-Cont	2.5	37.5	37.5	2.5	Stk	
Porsche Super	19	54	54	19	1/2	
Isky Porsche 103A	30	71	70	30	Full Race	.325

TABLE III

Iskenderian recommends the 2B grind if you are using the stock VW heads and the 2J grind for Okrasa, Porsche, and other free breathing types.

In addition, for the 5000 rpm range, heftier valve springs are needed to prevent valve float. Two sets of springs are available. The cheapest springs give about 25 per cent more push and are a "stock" heavy duty spring supplied by many foreign auto parts places. The Beck Distributing Company is the U.S. importer. These sell for approximately $3.00 a set and work nicely up to 5000 rpm even with the Okrasa and the 2J cam. For higher speeds or valves larger than the Okrasa more push is needed, and Iskenderian makes a good set of silicon-chrome steel springs for $12.00 a set. These have the added advantage of fewer coils, which allow spacers between the spring and the head to build up to whatever pressure you desire. However, with these springs you also need special Chromoly steel spring retainers at $7.00 a set, also made by Iskenderian. Experience has shown that the standard retainers will not withstand the extra pressure of the Iskenderian heavy duty springs.

Remarkably enough, these more radical cams have not caused any extra wear on the cam lobes, which speaks well for the original engine design and the engineering behind the Iskenderian grinds.

By the time this book is printed other cam grinds will be available and the manufacturers will no doubt send you information upon request.

THE TOP END

MUFFLER AND EXHAUST SYSTEM

The VW exhaust system can be one of the most efficient, because of low back pressure, but silencing is the main problem. Stock muffler silencing depends chiefly on two exhaust pipes protruding from the ends of the muffler which work something like gun silencers. In doing an efficient job of silencing considerable back pressure is built up within the muffler.

	Minimum Back Pressure in PSI
Stock VW engine and muffler at top speed, 3700 rpm	1.5
Stock VW muffler with 60 hp modified engine, 5000 rpm	3.0
Stock VW engine and muffler with silencing material removed, 3700 rpm	.75
Modified 60 hp engine with new free-flowing muffler, 5000 rpm	.25

TABLE IV
VW MUFFLER BACK PRESSURE

Table IV shows the back pressure of a stock VW muffler with various engine modifications. A good exhaust system should show zero back pressure at everything but top speed. The exhaust porting of the VW heads is satisfactory with an individual port for each cylinder but the muffler definitely needs improving.

The simplest way of relieving the back pressure on the later model twin pipe models is to remove the silencing material inside the pipes. This gives a 30 per cent increase in flow area, which removes most of the back pressure. The noise increase, however, is pretty violent and gives a raucous, tinny sound neither pleasant nor powerful.

The Advanced Car Specialties Co. in Toronto, Canada makes a set of taper tips selling for $13.95 that can easily be installed in place of the standard pipes. However, these do not give much silencing and have a "live" exhaust note.

THE TOP END

Many muffler specialty shops exist in this country, but as yet none markets a special low-back-pressure muffler.

Several good foreign jobs are available and at the top of the list is the Abarth Company represented by Fisher Products Corporation in New York. Two models are available. The A-100 is a universal model that will fit all VW's including the Karmann-Ghia. The A-200 model is designed for the 1956 and later stock models, with two tail pipes.

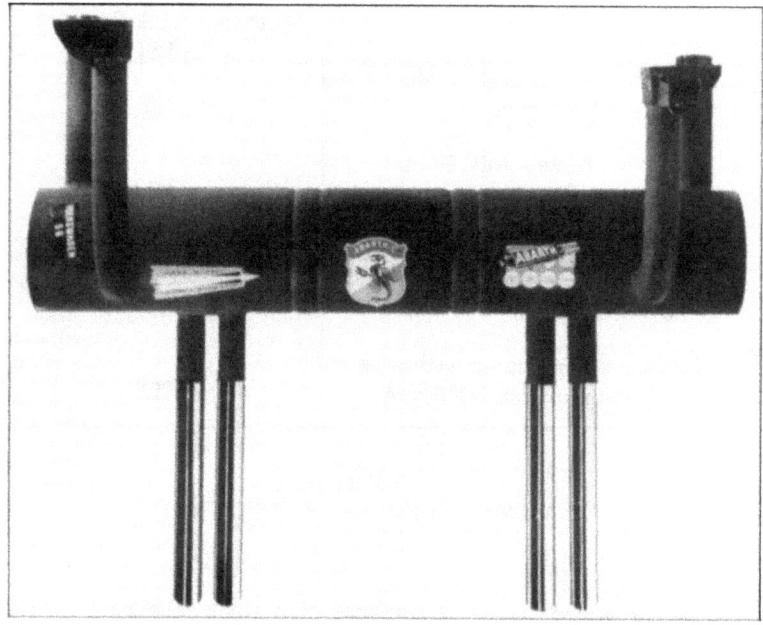

The Abarth muffler is typical of the zero-back-pressure type available for Volkswagen adding power potential.

Up to 1956, stock VW's had a single tail pipe leaving the muffler. Dual tail pipes were adopted for the 1956 models, but don't let this fool you. The stock duals have about the same outlet opening as the singles used before, and both build up plenty of back pressure at high speed.

Table IV shows the improvement that can be expected by changing the muffler only. These data are furnished by the Abarth people and indicates that a good muffler is definitely worth the investment.

Special VW mufflers sell for $33 to $35 but remember, this includes the whole exhaust system. To replace the exhaust system on other cars costs from $30 to $130 so that you can see the VW is outstanding in this department.

SECTION SIX
THE BOTTOM END

As noted previously the bottom end includes the pistons, rods, crankshaft, and bearings.

CRANKSHAFT

By now the word is around and it is an established fact, unfortunately proven hundreds of times, that the crankshaft is the prime weakness when souping the VW. In order not to bring the wrath of the VW factory down upon our heads we will establish here and now that the crankshaft seems completely adequate for the job for which it was intended. Stock VW's whose owners observe the factory red-lines have never been known to have a crankshaft breakage. But soup up a VW and head for those high revs without touching the crank, and powie; "Should I put it in a bag for you, lady?"

Fortunately, VW crank breakage seems to be concerned with fatigue failure. If it were a matter of not having enough strength for the stresses encountered at any time, under the worst conditions, then we would have to start from scratch with a new crank design.

The highest stresses on all the moving parts in an engine occur at the highest rpm and are due primarily to reciprocating motion. The faster the rods and pistons have to be whipped back and forth by the crankshaft the higher the stresses become.

One can verify this experimentally by rolling a heavy object back and forth on a smooth table top. At very low speed it is possible to roll a rather heavy object across the table with little resistance. As you speed up your hand you will notice more and more resistance, due to inertia. The faster it moves, the more force is required to move it, and it seems to get heavier.

During low speed operation the reciprocating forces on the rods and crank are small and the combustion forces from the pistons predominate. The combustion forces are dependent on the BMEP and since that is approximately constant throughout the speed range the combustion forces change little. The reciprocating forces, however, depend on speed and are the primary limiting factor as far as maximum engine speed is concerned.

As observed before, reciprocating stresses depend upon the speed that the pistons and rods are whipped back and forth. The absolute

THE BOTTOM END

speed or piston velocity is a measure of the stresses on the crank. Since a piston travels twice the stroke in one revolution, piston velocity is equal to two times the stroke times the rpm. An engine with a three inch stroke has a piston speed in feet per minute exactly one-half the engine rpm.

Present day rule-of-thumb design allows piston speeds up to 2500 feet per minute for continuous cruising power and up to 3500 feet per minute intermittently for maximum power.

The VW with a stock stroke of 2.52 inches (64mm) reaches 2500 feet per minute at 5950 rpm and 3500 feet per minute at 8350 rpm.

These numbers show that when we hop up the VW to put out maximum power between 5000 and 5500 rpm, we are not overstressing the bottom end. They also show how conservatively the engine was designed and why the factory can recommend cruising the cars at wide-open throttle all day long. At top speed, 3500 to 3700 rpm, the stock engine is only turning about 1500 feet per minute which indicates that it is practically loafing.

Even when we go to 5000 rpm the engine is still doing only 2100 feet per minute so that we can still cruise wide open if we desire.

VW gearing is not correct to obtain 5000 rpm in fourth gear but for climbing hills we can hold it in third gear up to 65 miles per hour without overstressing.

This is where the well known theoretical cruising speed of the VW comes out to be 120 miles per hour. Although the crank may be perfectly happy at 120, it would take about 125 horsepower, and more nerve than a used-car salesman, to hit that speed.

Of course most of this is purely hypothetical because whenever you hop up a VW and do not modify the crank nor use a stronger special crank, you can eventually expect a crank failure. The exact reasons are not known but probably are related to the fact that the crank is so lightly loaded that little care need be exercised in fabrication and balancing. Precision balancing usually shows that the stock crank and other parts are far from ideal for high speed operation.

Investigations by the Judson supercharger company have indicated that broken cranks have been the result of forging with too low metal temperatures. Regardless of the reasons, as long as the cranks do not break immediately but only after several thousand miles of hard driving we know that the break is a fatigue failure and can be prevented.

Fatigue failures are common with parts that are subject to high alternating stresses such as crankshafts, connecting rods, and valve springs. They start with a small, microscopic crack in the most

THE BOTTOM END

highly stressed region. Continuous stressing works the crack deeper and deeper into the material until finally it is just too weak to hold up. Breakage may occur any time, even when your wife is just puttering to the grocery store. Fortunately this is an old problem and shot-peening the surface has been found to be a good solution. Many parts on racing cars, airplanes, and even some stock automobiles are shot-peened to increase their fatigue strength. Valve springs are often shot-peened because they are highly stressed and go through many millions of cycles during their lifetime.

Because fatigue failures are caused by the metal failing in tension, that is, it tends to pull apart and crack, shot-peening prevents this by putting a very thin layer of the surface metal under a high compressive stress. Peening is accomplished by actually shooting fine shot at the surface. Every little particle on the surface of the part winds up peened over and pushing against its "neighbor," thus resulting in a compressive stress. Since it is obvious that a crack cannot start except by the metal being under tension the fatigue strength is tremendously improved.

The stress that most metal parts will withstand under highly fatiguing conditions is usually about one-half that of static or non-moving parts. Shot-peening restores the strength very close to the static value so that 100 per cent improvement in strength is common.

Before we embark on the shot-peening route we have to make sure that the parts do not already have fatigue cracks in them, and so we should have them magnafluxed. Magnafluxing is a way of magnetically inspecting for minute cracks and is usually quite inexpensive.

The crankshaft and four rods can usually be magnafluxed for a maximum of $5.00 and often cheaper. Aircraft engine repair shops can do magnafluxing or will tell you where it can be done. If the crankshaft and rods pass magnaflux inspection then we should cart the crank and rods, pistons, flywheel, clutch, and also the fan pulley over to the balancers. Be sure to include all of the little miscellaneous bolts, nuts, washers, keys, wrist pins, timing gear, and spacers as it has to be assembled just as it is when operating to be properly balanced.

Balancing is a very delicate job that must be done on precision electronic equipment costing thousands of dollars. There is no such thing as do-it-yourself balancing unless you have the exact equipment required. Balancing usually costs about $25 for the parts listed above, and every large city has one or more shops that can do this accurately.

THE BOTTOM END

Next and last is shot-peening the crank and rods, which again is not a do-it-yourself item. However, most every large city has at least one shot-peening shop which does cranks and connecting rods for other engines, so that there should be no problem with the VW.

Some hop-up shops specialize in complete "balance assemblies" which include all of the work listed above on your parts, or on an exchange basis.

At present most "hop-up shops" cater strictly to American products but more and more are catering to the foreign car market.

The other route to better crank stength is to buy a new stronger crank especially designed to take the added stresses. There are three ways to proceed, but right now only two of these seem to be practical. Since a special crank is needed and it is no more expensive to make a crank half an inch one way or the other, we can take advantage of this and increase the stroke at the same time.

Increasing the stroke increases the piston displacement with a resulting increase in power. If we can keep up with the piston displacement and cram more mixture into the cylinders in the same proportion as before, the power will go up exactly the same amount as the displacement.

Here we again follow the path pioneered by the model 356 Porsche. The first thing that Dr. Porsche did when souping up the VW engine for use in the Porsche was to adopt a longer stroke crankshaft. The Porsche crank from the 1300 to 1600 series has a 2.91 inch stroke (74mm) which is close to the limit that you can put in the crankcase. "Super" engines have a roller bearing crank but the stroke remains the same.

Heading the list of special cranks is the Okrasa 1300 cc stroker kit imported by the European Motor Products Co. Piston displacement is increased 94 cc., from 1192 to 1286, a 7.9 per cent increase. Compression ratio goes from the stock 6.6 to 7.5 to 1 if nothing else is changed. It is made from forged high tensile strength chrome alloy steel and has 5|16 inch deeper webs at the weakest section, betwen the front two throws.

When increasing the stroke one always encounters the problem of pistons being pushed higher in the cylinders. Most stroker kits need special pistons, called stroker pistons, that have the pin located higher on the skirt so that the top of the piston will remain in the same relative position with respect to the head and valves, and not cause interference problems. The Okrasa kit gets around this neatly by including spacers that are inserted under the cylinders boosting the cylinders, head and all, the required amount.

THE BOTTOM END

This Okrasa stroker crankshaft will increase the Volkswagen's displacement to 1285 cc and boost its compression ratio to 7.5 to 1.

Naturally this modification can be used only with mild strokers and the VW type of air-cooled construction with detachable cylinders. Another bonus for owning a VW.

The increase in stroke of the Okrasa is 5 millimeters, 0.20 inch, which is just half-way between the Porsche and the VW. The price of the Okrasa kit is $137.50 and includes all necessary parts and instructions.

Installation is straight-forward, with the following points to note:
1. Large spacers must be installed between the cylinder barrels and the crankcase.
2. Small spacers must be inserted in the push rods for extension.
3. Pistons must be cut away to clear crank and rods. Use small hand grinder or file.

If the facilities of a machine shop or lathe are handy an alternate method which can be used is to cut the top of the pistons back .110 inch from the top on each side. Taper the cut on a straight line so that nothing will be removed from the center and the top

THE BOTTOM END

The Okrasa stroker crank fits the VW case perfectly. No alteration needed on the case. No special tools, other than those normally required to do the engine assembly.

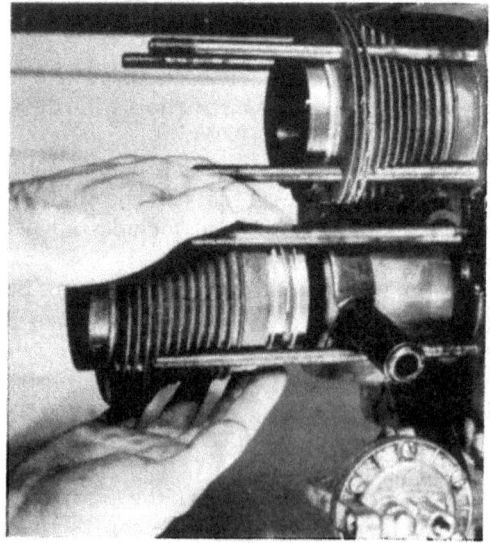

Use a gasket on each side of cylinder spacer. Install cylinder using ring compressor.

THE BOTTOM END

Note Spacer under cylinder. Install cylinder head and complete installation as on standard engine.

of the piston will look slightly conical. If this is done the spacers under the cylinders and the push rods will not be needed.

If nothing else is changed at the same time the Okrasa crank will give an 8 per cent boost in displacement and a 4 per cent boost in compression ratio, netting a 12 per cent gain in torque and power up to about 3500 rpm. Above this the restricted breathing of the stock VW intake system nullifies any increase.

A second good stroker kit is made by the Weber Tool Co. and comes in two different models, ¼ inch and ½ inch stroker. The cranks are machined from a cast billet and include the maximum strength webs that can be installed in the VW crankcase. Both kits include stroker pistons, balanced rods, new rod bushings, and piston rings. The ¼-inch kit increases the displacement 118 cc to 1310 cc (79.8 cu. ins) and sells for $199.50 with exchange rods. The ½-inch stroker kit increases the displacement 236 cc to 1427 cc (86.9 cu. ins.) and sells for $237.50. The ½-inch kit, however, includes a special reground camshaft which is not included with the ¼-inch kit. The difference in price can be accounted for by the camshaft alone so that you can see that it does not cost you any more to go the whole route.

THE BOTTOM END

The camshaft is necessary with the larger stroke since it has to be reground specially to clear the crankshaft. In fact the rods have to be cut away even on the short stroker because of this problem.

The special stroker pistons included also take care of a little power increase by upping the stock compression ratio from 6.6 to 8.0. Using the formula presented in Section   torque and power increase from this effect alone is over 5 per cent.

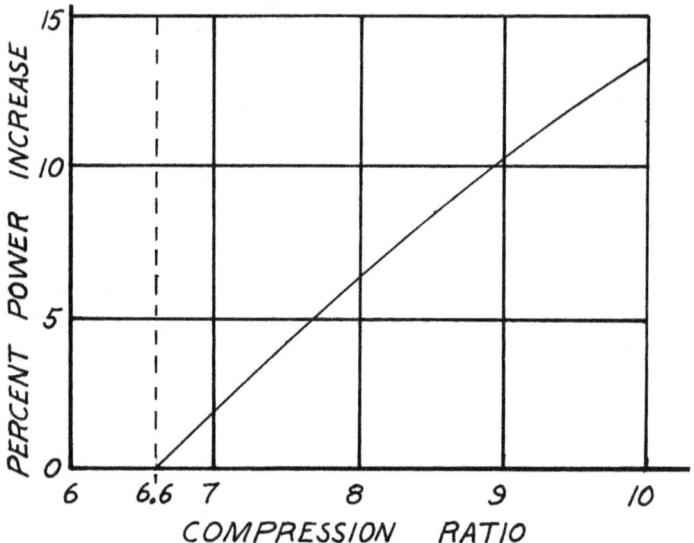

This chart shows the effect of increasing the compression ratio in the stock Volkswagen engine, using 6.6 to 1 ratio as the base and showing that with a 8.5 to 1 ratio the power is raised about 8 per cent.

Increasing the stroke increases the displacement and improves the torque and power in direct proportion at the lower rpm's. The ¼-inch stroker kit will give a 10 per cent increase plus the 5 per cent compression effect for a total of 15 per cent increase. The ½-inch kit will give a 20 per cent increase plus the 5 per cent to equal a good healthy 25 per cent increase in torque and power at the lower rpm's.

The third approach to increasing the stroke is to install a Porsche crank in the VW case. The Porsche crank has the same rod journal center distances and the same main bearing sizes as the VW. The rod bearings, however, are larger and not interchangeable. The Porsche crank is obviously beefed up over the VW crank because of larger rod journals. This increases the overlap between the rod and main bearing areas on the crank giving it more strength.

THE BOTTOM END

Porsche rods may be substituted for VW rods but then pistons become a problem because special stroker pistons are needed which have the pin located high enough to allow both for the increased stroke and extra rod length. Pistons like these have been specially made but are not available on the open market. They look exactly like Porsche pistons with two rings above the pin and one ring below the pin. Porsche pistons will not do the job as they have too large a bore. The 1500 Porsche bore is 80 mm, and although the VW cylinders can be bored out to this size there is almost nothing left of the cylinder wall. If you do assemble an engine this way do not trust the balancing on the Porsche rods and crank. They are generally out of true balance like the VW.

Bearings

Bearings seem to give little problem on the VW. The main bearings are made of aluminum which is now used in engines that get very heavy service. Stock rod bearings are good and are recommended for all "street" engines. Vandervell replacements are available from almost any local foreign parts dealer for competition.

All crankshaft and rod bearings are of the replaceable insert type so that no wear is experienced by the case or rods. The exception is the camshaft which rides directly in the magnesium crankcase, but these surfaces show little wear until the engine has gone over 100,000 miles.

Cylinders and Pistons

VW cylinders are made of a good hard grade of cast iron and are very durable even on souped-up engines. The cylinders may be bored out about a maximum of 2 mm (.080 inch) without running into any problems. This allows the 77 mm bore pistons, used on 1954 and later cars, to be bored out to within 1 mm of the 1500 Porsche size, 80 mm. Do not try for this last millimeter with the VW cylinders as the wall just gets too thin. The problem lies more in the boring than the running. That last millimeter will give you a 2 per cent increase in performance and a 100 per cent increase in headaches.

Before 1954 the stock bore was 75 mm and these may either be bored out their allotted 2 mm or may be replaced with the later model cylinders. When replacing the earlier ones with the later cylinders the hole into which they "spigot" in the crankcase has

THE BOTTOM END

to be enlarged about .080 of an inch because the outside diameter is 2 mm larger, the same as the inside diameter. Leave between .005 and .010 inch clearance between the cylinder and the crankcase. The best thing to do is to obtain the cylinders first, then take them to the machine shop that does the boring so that they can be measured accurately. *NOTE: Be sure to tell them that the case is magnesium so that they can take the proper precautions when machining.* The new bore should follow the old bore exactly so that the center distance between the holes remains the same, otherwise the cylinders will be tilted or warped and will leak in the heads and bind with the pistons.

The pre-1954 cylinder heads also have to be bored out to the new size, .080 inch larger, but the best thing to do is to throw them in the nearest trash barrel. There are several sizes of induction passages that have been used on automobiles. In descending order of size they are: large, medium, small, extremely small, microscopic, and pre-1954 VW. The only sensible thing is to replace the old heads with the later model or Okrasa. The Okrasa heads are not made to fit the earlier cylinders so that if you are going to Okrasa you must change to the late model.

When boring the VW cylinders they must not be clamped in the jaws of a regular lathe chuck but must be held in a special fixture that bolts them down in exactly the same manner as in the engine. This may be done either on a lathe, or with a regular engine boring-bar, but in any case the special fixture must be used.

VW dealers are a good source for old cylinders if you want to rebore to the maximum oversize. Since the VW dealers are required to use new factory cylinders when the stock cylinders are worn out, they usually have some of the old ones lying around in the corners that they will sell for a nominal price. Basically this is a good policy for the average owner who is not interested in extra performance, as the price for new cylinders is very reasonable and the factory retains control over every part that goes into the cars. A complete set of stock pistons, cylinders, rings, pins, all new, cost only about $65 at any VW dealer or independent foreign parts supply house.

Boring the cylinders 2 mm (.080) oversize will increase the displacement of an engine with stock stroke 5 per cent with a corresponding increase in torque and power where breathing is not restricted. Since new pistons are always needed with a rebore we can take advantage of this and wind up with an increase in compression ratio also. However, here, we enter into an area that can become quite complicated for someone who is not an automotive engineer.

THE BOTTOM END

Increasing the displacement only, with no other change, will automatically increase the compression ratio. The effect is almost the same as the displacement increase, that is, a 5 per cent increase in displacement will produce a 5 per cent increase in compession ratio. With stock pistons the 2 mm increase in bore will increase the compression ratio from the stock 6.6 to 6.9. If we buy pistons that will give a stock engine a compression ratio of 7.5, then with the 2 mm overbore the compression ratio will be 7.8 to 1.

Increases in stroke aggravate the situation so that you must be extremely careful and compute your compression ratio exactly as given by the formula.

If we use a 2 mm overbore and wind up with a compression ratio of 7.5 to 1 then we have a 5 per cent increase due to displacement and a 4 per cent increase in power and torque, due to compression ratio, with a net gain of 9 per cent. A compression ratio of 8.5 to 1 would add another 4 per cent for a net gain of 13 per cent and would require the use of premium fuel. However, remember the use of premium fuel ups your gas bill by about 25 per cent and obviously nullifies the economy advantages of the VW.

Overbore pistons are not available from VW dealers but may be purchased from independent foreign car parts dealers, and special piston manufacturers such as Jahns. Hepolite pistons are available up to .060 oversize through parts dealers, while companies like Jahns will make almost any size that you want.

It is desirable to use pistons for air-cooled engines that have a variable expansion skirt such as a "T" slot, but it is not absolutely necessary. Hepolite pistons with the "T" slot can run in an unblown engine at the factory recommended clearances of .0015 to .0025 inches. Solid skirt pistons should run .003 to .004 inches. If a blower is to be used, add at least .001 to these dimensions.

Because aluminum pistons operating in cast iron cylinders tend to expand considerably more than cast iron, it is clear why these clearances are needed. The extra temperatures experienced with a blower only aggravate these conditions and require more clearance.

It is interesting to note, at this point, that the early Porsche aluminum cylinders up to 1954 will fit the VW crankcase if the cylinder holes are bored out to the correct size. Bolt spacing and the vertical height of the mating surfaces are exactly the same *(remember they used the VW crankcase)*. It is necessary to remove the top fin on the Porsche cylinders and of course the heads have to be bored larger too. As Porsche aluminum pistons and cylinders sell for about $250 a set, only people with money trees drive VW's

THE BOTTOM END

with these installed. Little is to be gained unless you are driving in competition. It is interesting to observe that the 1958 Porsches use cast iron cylinders like the VW. These will not fit the VW since they are made to fit on the three piece, strictly Porsche, crankcase which has wider cylinder bolt spacing than the VW.

Except for the crankshaft, the bottom end of the Volkswagen is quite rugged, and needs little modification.

Shot-peening the stock crank or using a new "beefier" crank together with balancing of crank, rods, pistons and clutch puts the bottom end in good shape for many carefree miles.

Stan Mott

These modifications are certainly not recommended by the factory but the hot rodder has his own ideas.

SECTION SEVEN
ASSEMBLY AND DISASSEMBLY

This chapter is intended to guide those who will work on the VW engine with few of the tools recommended by the factory. You may be a real competition enthusiast and have your engine apart every week, in which case you might find only one or two little hints that you didn't think of yourself. On the other hand there are many VW owners who are pretty good amateur mechanics but probably have never torn into their engine because the factory propaganda has frightened them out.

Have you put in a set of rings, or torn the engine down to the last bolt and nut, having the crankshaft reground and cylinders rebored in a Ford or Chevy? If you have, then you can do the same thing on the VW engine. The same basic principles apply but the engine is constructed differently and a little more care is needed in some areas.

In fact, after you have torn into your engine two or three times you will think it is one of the easiest engines in the world to work on. Can you think of any other car of comparable size in which you can remove the engine and have it on the *work bench*, tearing into it, only one hour after you started? VW mechanics can remove an engine in 15 to 20 minutes without working too hard. Using a stopwatch, a group of mechanics were observed to remove an engine in a little under six minutes. If this became a national fad, it is easy to see where we would have VW engine removal contests. During long races you could burn up several engines and then change them in one or two minutes, just like tires at Indianapolis. Oh, well!

Naturally you have to have some tools that are different for working on the VW. As a starter the following wrench sizes are absolutely necessary as they are constantly recurring:

Box ends, open ends, and sockets:
10 mm.
14 mm.
17 mm.

It is useful to have these in the complete range of 8 mm to 19 mm.

In addition the following wrenches will be needed for specialized parts of the engine:

36 mm socket.
250 ft lb torque wrench or smaller torque wrench with range extender.
10 mm Allen-type socket for head bolts.

ASSEMBLY AND DISASSEMBLY

These wrenches are available from some American companies but the best selection is usually obtainable from German importers. Imported sockets can be obtained with American drive sizes such as ⅜, ½, and ¾ inch.

Another necessary item is a factory workshop manual. Dealers are usually skimpy with these following the "party line" of discouraging do-it-yourselfers.

We will assume that you have a copy of the service manual and will not duplicate instructions from it. We will deviate in a few cases where extensive tests have proved that a change may be made without any effect.

ENGINE REMOVAL

Remove engine as indicated in manual but drain oil *before* removal. No sheet metal has to be removed from the engine before removal from the car. Remove fan belt and all pulley parts from generator. Accessibility is easier if the deck lid is removed also.

It is easiest to lift the car with a chain hoist and use a floor jack under the engine. If a floor jack is not available make a dolly with small rollers to put under the engine. Build it up so that it does *not* clear the engine by an inch or two when the car is in its normal position. Lift the car up and set it gently back down with the dolly under the engine, supporting it. Pull back on the engine and if everything is disconnected, it will come loose easily. Lift the car about two feet in the air until the back clears the top of the fan housing, and roll out the engine.

Keep the engine centered exactly when removing or installing, or it will not clear. Take care that the engine is free at all times and not hanging up on the transmission shaft, distributor, carburetor, or generator.

ENGINE DISASSEMBLY

Disassemble according to the manual and note that everything including the fan pulley and flywheel has to be removed from the engine before the case can be split.

Flywheel removal requires the use of the 250 ft. lb. torque wrench. The factory tool for this is the largest torque wrench that you have ever seen and costs around $50. However, if you own or can borrow a 100 to 150 ft. lb. torque wrench, then a special torque wrench extension is available from the California Motor Engineering Company for only $7 that will extend the range of your torque wrench to the amount needed.

ASSEMBLY AND DISASSEMBLY

Torque is increased by the ratio of the new total length, with the extender, to the length of the torque wrench alone. Thus if a 15 inch length is added to a 15 inch torque wrench, then a reading of 100 ft. lb. will mean an actual torque at the flywheel nut of 200 ft. lb. Figure 9 shows the extender in use during tightening.

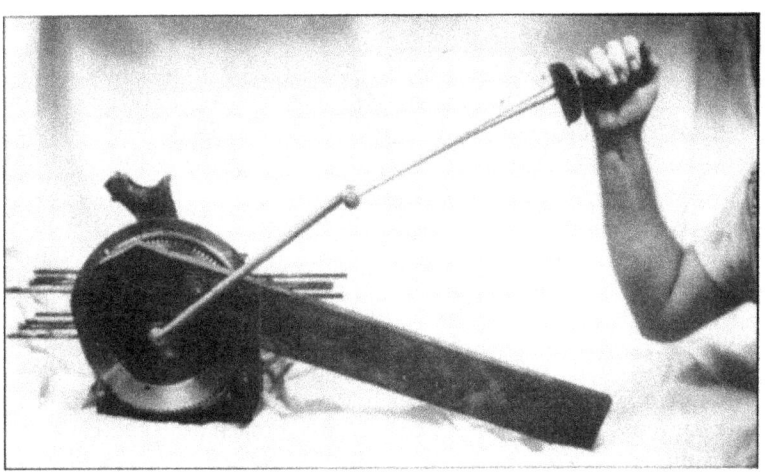

FIGURE 9. *Tightening the VW flywheel nut with a 100 ft. lb. torque wrench and extended range adapter. Note that the wooden 2-by-4 bolted to the flywheel eliminates the need for a beefy assembly stand.*

When exerting this much torque on an engine as light as the VW a problem arises as how to hold the engine and the best way is shown in Figure 9. Bolt a stout 2 x 4 board to the flywheel about the same length as the total torque wrench, using three of the clutch pressure plate bolts and holes. Counterbore the 2 x 4 for the bolts.

With the engine on a large flat hard surface such as a work bench or cement floor and the board resting so that the floor resists the torque, loosen the flywheel nut. When the flywheel nut is removed, repeated gentle blows with a soft hammer all around the periphery of the flywheel will loosen it, and it comes right off.

The oil pump may be removed without a puller by firmly but gently prying with a large screw driver. Do not hammer a screw driver or any tool into the case when removing parts or splitting it. Prying parts off the magnesium crankcase must be done easily so that no machined surfaces are scratched or marred.

The pins are usually a light press fit in the pistons and have to be heated for removal. A good way to do this is with a small butane or propane torch such as made by Lenk. It can be purchased at

ASSEMBLY AND DISASSEMBLY

any hardware store for a few dollars and works nicely both for removing and installing the pistons. The pistons will not go through the sides of the case, so do not attempt to split the case before removal of the pistons. It helps to have a special pusher for pin removal that has a pilot which fits inside of the pin. In any case, do not pound the pin out unless you can support the piston adequately so that the rod does not take the force and bend.

The best method is to turn the engine so that the crankshaft is vertical while removing the pistons. Then gravity will be on your side and the pins should drop right out. Caution:—Use wet rags to cover the oily areas near the torch so that the entire operation does not go up in one big ball of black smoke.

With everything off, the crankcase comes apart very easily *when all of the bolts holding it together are removed*. This cannot be overemphasized. The first time that you take a VW case apart you will be amazed at all of the small bolts, large bolts, medium sized bolts, and studs holding it together. Lay it down with the crankshaft horizontal, and firmly tap the main bearing studs that come through on the right side (facing forward) of the engine with a soft hammer. If after two or three taps on each stud the case does not split, clean away some more dirt and look for more bolts. Regardless of how tempting it is to pound something sharp between the two halves *do not do it*. Double-, triple-, quadruple-check for all of the bolts. Each time you go around you will find one more.

After the crankcase is about ¼ inch apart support the engine on its left side and remove the right side by pulling straight up. A gentle tap with a soft hammer and the crank and cam will stay in the left side.

After removal of the crank and cam, remove the five little locating pins for the main bearings with a pair of pliers. This is just to keep them from getting lost as they fall out on occasion when you are cleaning the crankcase. Four are on one side, and one is on the other side (the split main bearing).

Although the manual mentions heating the gears for removal from the crankshaft this is usually not practical and a gear puller has been found to be entirely satisfactory. Pull on the bottom of the inner-most gear with a sturdy puller. This is a hard pull and a cheap "weak sister" job just will not do it. If you do not have a good gear puller they may be rented for a nominal fee from most parts supply houses or automobile machine shops. If you wish to go nuts at this point just forget to remove the snap ring holding the gears on.

ASSEMBLY AND DISASSEMBLY

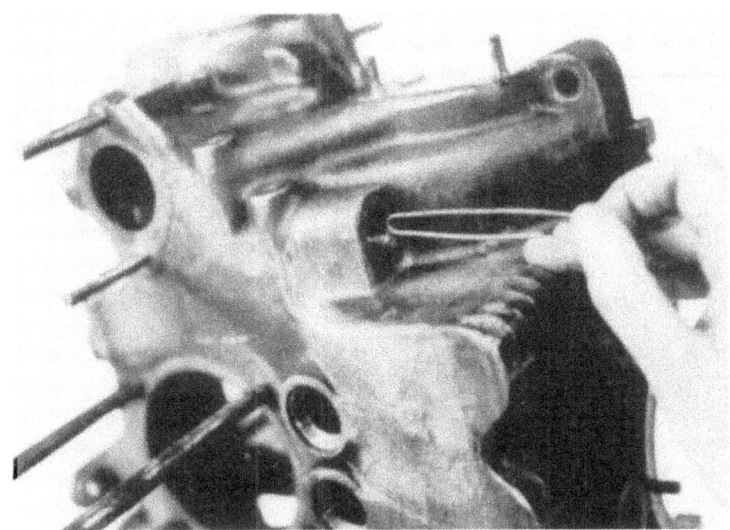

FIGURE 10. *This picture shows a special bent wire tool for removing the oil pressure relief valve of the Volkswagen.*

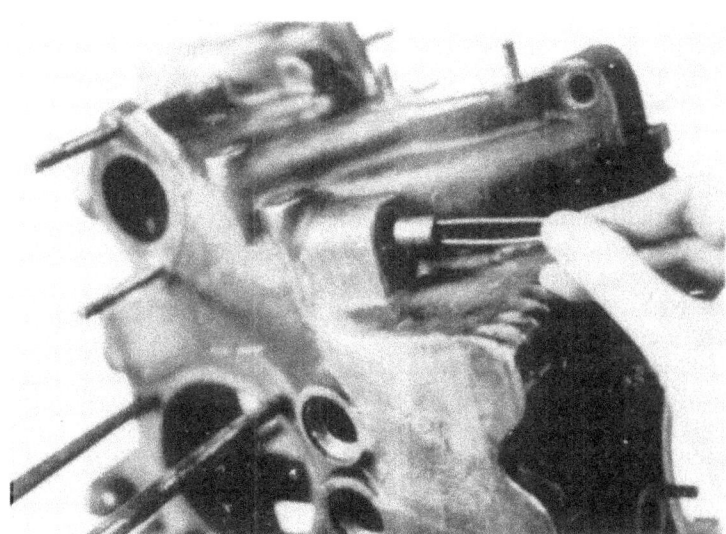

FIGURE 10A. *Removal of the oil pressure relief valve can be accomplished by use of the bent wire tool.*

ASSEMBLY AND DISASSEMBLY

The engine should be just about completely disassembled by now, except for the cylinder heads. Valves may be removed from the heads in a conventional manner using an overhead- valve-type spring compressor. The valves may also be removed by using a drill press. In fact they can be removed just by supporting the valve head underneath and pushing down on the retaining washer by hand, using a short piece of tubing. Cut the tubing away on each side and pry in with a small screw driver and remove the half-moon keepers.

VW's are hard on valve guides and they usually need replacing after 30,000 to 40,000 miles. The factory method is to shrink the new guides in liquid air before inserting. This is fine if you have any liquid air in your shop. All I have is the hot gaseous type. The next best thing, and just as good, is the special replacement guides that European Motor Products Company sells. These are a drive fit at room temperature but the use of a special Led Plate compound makes them slip in as smooth as glass, with no galling.

The only item remaining is the removal from the crankcase of the oil pressure regulator. Note its position (from the manual) and unscrew the cap with a very large screw driver or a chisel sharpened to fit into the screw slot. With either one a six- to eight-inch crescent wrench is usually needed. Remove the spring and bend a heavy piece of wire into the shape shown in Figure 10. The valve body is hollow and the wire may be pushed in. If it is a good tight fit the valve body may be withdrawn without much trouble. Oiling the passage with a light penetrating oil will facilitate removal.

CLEANING AND INSPECTION

Clean all of the parts that are to be re-used and inspect to see if the parts are within the recommended factory tolerances as listed in the service manual. Blast out all of the oil passages in the crankcase with air or water to make sure that they are clean and free. Blow air through the push rods to make sure that the oil passage is not clogged. This is not a large passage so do not expect too much, but make sure that some air gets through. Clean off all the old paper and sealant by scraping gently and using a strong solvent such as laquer thinner. Gently glide a large flat file over the mating surfaces of the two crankcase pieces removing any small burrs, providing an absolutely flat and clean surface for perfect sealing. You will notice that there is no gasket at this joint, but it never leaks if treated with care.

ENGINE ASSEMBLY

We will assume that you have the parts that you want to put into your engine grouped together. The major points of assembly vary slightly with the equipment used.

Assembly is practically the reverse of disassembly. Start with the crankshaft, installing the main bearing cam drive and distributor drive gears, in that order. If a fiber timing gear has been used, with not more than 20,000 miles on it, and there are no obvious signs of wear, then the old cam drive gear can be reinstalled. If the *used* cam drive gear rode against a *metal* timing gear, then a new cam gear must be installed if a new timing gear is to be used. If the same metal timing gear is to be installed use the old cam drive gear. If you are confused then just buy a new cam drive gear. They cost only about $2.50.

Replace the distributor drive gear on the shaft with the bronze model that is used in the Porsche. They are exactly the same except for material. Examine the distributor drive shaft with which it mates in the case, for wear, and if the teeth are sharp replace it with the stock VW part.

Before assembling the No. 3 bearing on the shaft, put all of the bearings in their respective positions in the side of the crankcase that has an aligning dowel pin for each bearing, and mark with a pencil the depth of the bearing. This helps to position the bearings correctly when installing the shaft.

We are now ready to assemble the gears on the crankshaft. Heat the two gears in an oven for about one half hour at 350 degrees F. Make sure that the gears are clean and free of solvent so that you do not have an explosion. Use a clean Pyrex bowl so that they can be carried to the point of assembly without cooling too much. The gears should have reached a temperature by this time to fall on the shaft with plenty of clearance. Note the correct order of assembly with spacer. Install a new snap ring after you are sure that the gears are all the way on the shaft. The cam drive gear only goes on one way. The two little timing dots point toward the pulley end of the shaft.

We are now ready to set the end play of the crankshaft. This is a very important point of assembly but not too difficult. Number 1 main bearing absorbs all end thrust. Clearance is adjusted by shimming between the bearing and the flywheel. The following five different sizes of shims are available from VW dealers for this adjustment. Dimensions are given both in millimeters and inches for ease of computing:

ASSEMBLY AND DISASSEMBLY

Millimeters	Inches
.30	.0118
.32	.0126
.34	.0134
.36	.0142
.38	.0150

Slip the No. 1 main bearing on the flywheel end of the shaft and bolt on the flywheel to the required torque. Be sure to include the small paper gasket and have the mating surfaces perfectly clean. Check the clearance between the bearing and the flywheel with a feeler gauge. Without shims this clearance is usually between .030 and .040 inches. See Figure 11.

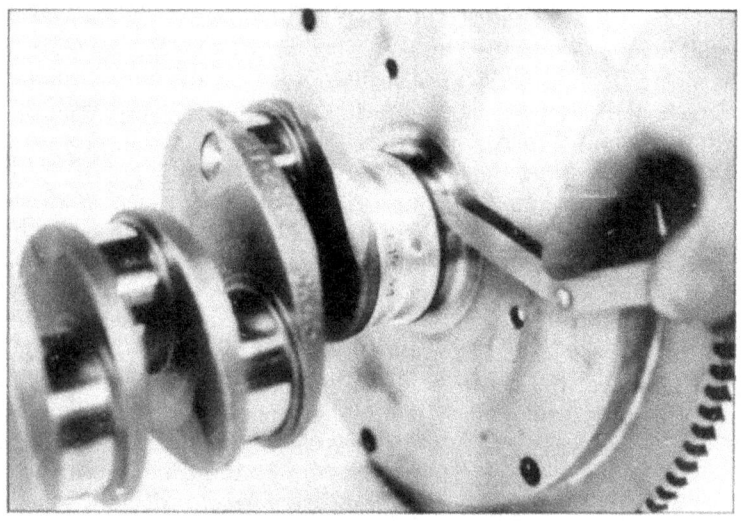

FIGURE 11. *Checking the No. 1 main bearing for end play, using a feeler gauge.*

Compute the shim thickness necessary to give a .003 to .005 clearance, using whatever combination of the five sizes is needed. Always try for the .003 so that it will give maximum life before worn to the limit of .006.

As an example assume that the clearance measured with the feeler gauge is .038. Required shim thickness is then .035. The closest we can come is three of the .30 mm shims for a total thickness of .0348. Clearance will then be .0032 which is within the required range.

ASSEMBLY AND DISASSEMBLY

Remove the flywheel from the shaft, and install the required shims. Reassemble, torquing as before, and check the clearance. You should be able to insert a .003 feeler gauge but not a .004 feeler gauge.

If you have trouble, repeat until you are satisfied that the clearance is correct. Always push the shaft toward the flywheel end when measuring, and always use shims that are not worn. Worn shims have a step in them and give an erroneous measurement.

This method of determining the axial shaft clearance is slower than the factory method but eliminates the dial indicator and special fixture.

Remove the flywheel and assemble the rods on the crank as per instructions in the manual. Firm taps with a soft hammer will align them properly during tightening. They must fall freely by their own weight when properly installed. Do not forget to lock them with a center punch.

The shaft and rods should now look like Figure 12 and are ready for installation in the case.

FIGURE 12. *Volkswagen crankshaft assembly is shown here just before it is inserted in the crankcase.*

The crank assembly is installed in the left side of the case. Install as per manual with all main bearings and oil slinger in place. After the shaft is set in place rotate the one-piece bearings until the dowel pins are properly aligned. Check to see that the rods on the first and third crank throws are through

ASSEMBLY AND DISASSEMBLY

the cylinder holes in the case. No errors are allowed in this operation. *If you do not have the dowel pins in their correct holes the bearings will be damaged beyond repair.* Parts that are left off cannot be added later, so check and double check.

FIGURE 12A. *Aligning the main VW bearings with dowel pins.*

Install the camshaft per manual and oil all bearings and gears.

Prepare the right hand case for assembly by coating the mating surface with liquid Aviation Permatex. Spread it very thin and evenly *taking care not to get any in the oil passages.* Inspect the mating surfaces of both sides to see if they are free of burrs, dirt, and chips.

Install a new oil seal in the left case with Permatex around the surface that is squeezed between the case halves. Also put Permatex around camshaft plug.

Assemble the right case to the left case by sliding it down over the bearing studs. Check the oil seal to make sure that it is square and firmly against the shoulder provided for it.

Install two nuts on the studs and tighten down until the surfaces touch. The crankshaft should rotate freely for a complete revolution with no dragging or binding. Install the rest of the bolts and nuts, and torque per manual. Paper washers are provided for main bearing studs to prevent oil leaks.

Check crankshaft rotation after final tightening. It should rotate freely with no intermittent catching or binding. Intermittent binding indicates burrs or chips on the cam gears.

ASSEMBLY AND DISASSEMBLY

Pistons are next. Stand the engine so that the crankshaft is vertical with the large flanged (front) end down. The pistons have to be installed first next to the flange. Put a circlip in each piston so that it will be on the underneath side when mounted on the rod, in this position.

If the pistons need to be heated for pin insertion use boiling water, a small propane torch such as made by Lenk, or an electric hot plate. The boiling water method requires that the pistons be heated in a pan of boiling water for two or three minutes prior to installation. This is a little awkward as the pistons cool rapidly leaving only a few seconds for pin insertion. However, with this method you are sure of not overheating the pistons.

If a torch is used the pistons may be put on the rods while heating. Play the torch all over the piston so that it is not overheated in any one spot. Two or three minutes is usually required with a Lenk-type torch. Insert the pin when it will go in freely with but little push.

Cylinders are next, with the paper gasket on bottom and copper gasket on the top end. Rings are a major problem as you will discover that no ordinary ring compressor will work. If the rings do not have any expanders behind them they can be worked in by hand, one at a time, as the cylinder is pushed over them. A good size chamfer is available at the bottom of the stock cylinders but if you have them bored out then you will have to make a new chamfer. Use a file and make it a good sixteenth-inch wide at about 45 degrees.

Hazlet makes a compressor for this job which is easy to use. If you are in a bind you can make one with a large hose clamp. Bend a piece of 1/16 thick aluminum wide enuogh to cover the rings into a circle. Put the aluminum around the rings and tighten the hose clamp around the aluminum. Tap the cylinder on, gently pushing the compressor to the bottom of the piston skirt while the rings slide into the cylinder. Cut the aluminum so that the ends do not quite touch when it is compressed around the rings.

When pushing a cylinder over a piston make sure that it does not hang up on the head studs, or you will break a fin. Cast iron is brittle, you know.

Next insert the little air baffles under the cylinders on each side. *Write yourself a note or hang them from your wrists with a piece of string.* In your anxiety to install the nice new gleaming heads you will surely forget them.

Install the heads according to the factory manual and any special instructions that might come with special heads you are using.

ASSEMBLY AND DISASSEMBLY

The following instructions apply to the Okrasa head kit only:
Install push rod covers with new rubber seals and install new Okrasa heads torquing down according to factory instructions.
Install cylinder sheet metal covers and note how cut has to be made to clear intake manifolds.
Using paper template furnished with kit cut out sheet metal to match intake manifolds. The sheet metal must fit tightly around the manifolds or excessive air leakage will occur. When fitting use the manifold gasket and check frequently. Do not rely on the paper template for final fit. Use tin snips, grinder, files (rotary if you can get one), blood, sweat, tears, and about four hours, for a good fit.
Braze or solder the throttle bell crank to the fan housing in the following manner:

> Carefully locate the position of the throttle bell crank on the fan housing. Move the bell crank and note the movement of the throttle wire that will be required to follow properly. The bell crank should be positioned for minimum wire drag on the sides, bottom, and top of its tube. The end of the tube has to be cut off leaving about one quarter inch protruding past the square stop. Mark the position of the bell crank by scratching lines two or three inches past the end of the mount for alignment when brazing. Clean to the bare metal that part of the fan housing where the soldering or brazing will occur. Braze or solder the bell crank to the fan housing. If you are using soft solder *tin* the fan housing and bell crank thoroughly first with acid type. Use a flame for soldering. The small Lenk propane torch is a neat outfit that costs only $3 to $4 and is quite useful around the shop. Soft solder must completely fill the joint between the bell crank and the fan housing for satisfactory results. Use plenty and fillet-in the edges of the joint.

Reposition coil using lower mounting threads for upper part of coil bracket. Drill hole and bolt for lower bracket. If space permits mount oil filter on fan housing.
Install fan housing. Cock the housing slightly to clear the manifolds. Use short 10 mm hex head bolts for sides.
Mount the ignition wire harness on the two lower bolts holding the fan cover to housing using loop clamps.
Mount carburetors and throttle linkage and adjust for equal opening and closing.

ASSEMBLY AND DISASSEMBLY

Drill a small hole through the throttle wire cover on the front side of the fan housing and insert a small cotter pin. This prevents the tube from coming out and jamming the bell crank.

Install engine in car, reversing the removal process, step-by-step. The engine has to be "cocked" to allow wider span of Okrasa carbs to enter engine compartment. Keep engine centered exactly or it will not clear properly.

When engine is lined up and in proper position put car in fourth gear and rock *gently* to synchronize clutch splines. When splines are lined up the engine will slip into place easily.

Install generator pulley, fan belt, and connect all gas and heater lines. Cut swaged fitting off end of throttle wire and clamp in bell crank fixture. Check for full throttle movement and adjust if necessary. The accelerator pedal should be against the full throttle stop on the floor when the carburetor butterflies are wide open.

Stan Mott

Mott's idea of how Walt Disney would soup a Volkswagen.

SECTION EIGHT

LUBRICATION

The lubrication system of the VW is as modern as a jet plane though the engine design is 25 years old. Full pressure is supplied to all of the main rod and cam bearings. Rockers are supplied oil through the push rods. The oil is cooled immediately after leaving the pump by a multitube cooler in the fan housing. The amount of oil flowing through the cooler is controlled by a remarkably simple three-way relief valve. When engine oil is cold the valve relieves the excess pressure, returning oil to the crankcase and allowing the primary flow of oil to bypass the cooler. However, as the oil warms up, an increasing amount flows through the cooler until at high temperature all the oil circulates through the cooler.

Oil is responsible for part of the cooling in any engine. In water-cooled engines the oil comes in contact with much of the water jacket during its travels, so that it gets cooled without a special cooler of its own. An air-cooled engine, however, doesn't have this feature, and must rely on a separate oil cooler.

Oil temperature in a VW can run quite high during full power operation on a hot day. It isn't uncommon for the oil to actually melt the soft solder used in the cooler during extreme conditions. Even stock VW's have had this problem.

Fortunately a good copper brazed cooler of the same type used on the Porsche is now available on the market for only $13.50. It replaces the stock cooler without any modifications, and is far superior, and is imported by Louis Pierlot of Inglewood, California. When you tear into your engine be it stock or souped-up, throw the old cooler away and install the new model. See Figure 13.

Another good thing to do to your engine whether stock or souped is to install a good oil filter. This insures your engine a clean supply of oil and adds about 40 per cent more capacity for better cooling. Several good ones are available. EMPI makes a "spin on" type that mounts neatly in the rear of the engine regardless of type of vehicle. Fram and Purolator make VW conversion kits which cost about $15 complete and are easy to install. If you have one of the last two you have the advantage of being able to purchase replacement elements at the nearest gas station almost anywhere in the world. The Fram and Purolater types may be mounted on the fan housing ala Porsche in the sedan only. K-G and Transporter models require firewall mounting which is occasionally awkward to service.

LUBRICATION

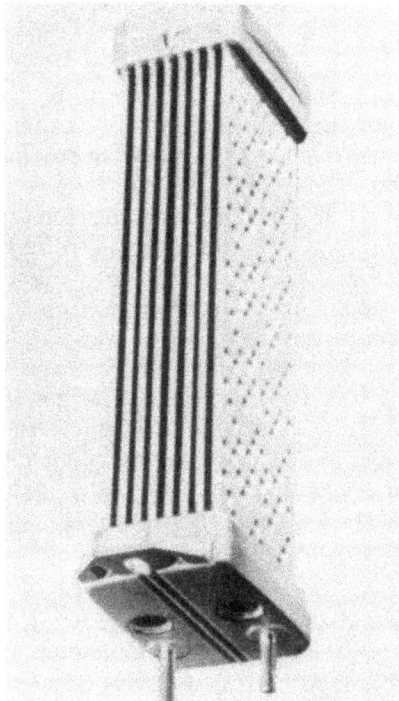

FIGURE 13. *The Pierlot oil cooler, imported for installation on high-performance VW's.*

Regardless of the type, make sure that you leave adequate clearance for cleaning and/or removal and that the deck lid closes without interference.

When it comes to the type of oil to use the VW owner has been treated to more confusion than a honey bear in a buzzer factory. Unfortunately the VW factory was slow in adopting the new advanced heavy duty oils. This led to the general opinion that these oils were harmful to the VW engine. Nothing could be further from the truth.

Extensive tests have shown that most wear on an engine occurs during stop and go around town driving. Oil dilution, acid formation, and sludge formation occur very rapidly when the engine is cold. Cylinder, piston, and bearing wear are accelerated by these conditions. Oddly enough it has been conclusively proved that the chemical wear from these conditions is many times the mechanical wear rate experienced, even when operating for sustained periods of high speed and power.

The main purpose behind the heavy duty (detergent) type oils is the resistance of the chemical attack on your engine and oil deterioration during the low temperature, critical period of driving.

LUBRICATION

One of the reasons undoubtedly for the long life of the VW engine is a couple of "built in" oil additives. First, being air-cooled the cylinder walls have no mass of water to be heated before they can leave the low temperature, high wear condition. Second, the magnesium crankcase has a tendency to neutralize acids that form in the oil.

Another recent advance has been the development of multi-range viscosity oils. Engine wear is further reduced by having oil in your engine that will flow readily to all of the smallest nooks and crannies providing good lubrication when cold, yet not thin out excessively when hot. These are readily available in SAE 10-30 and 20-40 formulations. An SAE 10-30 oil, for exmaple, will have the low viscosity of a 10 weight oil when starting cold but will have a viscosity as high as a 30-weight oil when warm. Since the VW engine has a wider range of operating temperatures than water cooled engines it seems that these oils are a "natural." SAE 10-30 is probably the best all-around oil while 20-40 would be most useful during extremely hot weather.

Another misconception which has crept into VW lore is that heavy duty oils ruin the aluminum main bearings. The thin film of oxide that forms on every piece of aluminum when first exposed to air is one of the most corrosion-resistant materials known. Pure aluminum is one of only a few materials that is used every day with highly reactive rocket propellants such as red fuming nitric acid, liquid oxygen, liquid fluorine, and hydrogen peroxide. Aluminum bearings are the only kind that stand up in diesel engines subject to extreme and highly corrosive conditions of highly sulfurized fuels. It is interesting to note that all diesel engines now use extreme heavy duty oils to combat the varnish and sludge generated by diesel fuels. Nuff said?

For racing purposes where the ultimate in direct lubricating properties is required straight mineral oils are still the best. Depending upon oil temperature and pressure use SAE 50 or 70. Spare the oil cooler by not racing your engine until the oil gets warm.

One more important point. Do not switch to heavy duty oils if you have been using straight mineral oil for very long. The cleaning power of the heavy duty oils breaks off the dirt and sludge accumulated in the recesses of the engine. These can clog the oil passages with disastrous results. If you have been using straight oils only a short time, less than 20,000 miles, change the oil every 200 to 300 miles two or three times before settling down to your regular schedule. VW dealers have special instructions for this operation.

SECTION NINE

IGNITION

The Bosch ignition system furnished with the VW is top quality and gives long and trouble-free service. It is entirely conventional in design, with a four lobe cam distributor rotating at one half crankshaft speed, feeding a spark every other revolution to a single spark plug in each cylinder. Firing order is 1-4-3-2.

Cars built after January 1954, have a vacuum and centrifugal advance built into the distributor. Before that time they incorporated the centrifugal advance only.

The centrifugal advance is used in all modern engines. It ignites the fuel in the cylinder earlier as the engine speeds up so that it will always be burned by the time the piston is ready to start down on the power stroke. Since the fuel-air mixture takes a definite time to ignite and burn it must be ignited sooner at high engine speed.

The vacuum advance is strictly a fuel economizer. During part-throttle operation such as steady cruising at 30 to 50 mph the vacuum mechanism advances the spark (fires earlier) even beyond the centrifugal setting. Since the fuel burns more slowly at reduced pressure, when the throttle is only partly open, ignition must be started even earlier to utilize the fuel most efficiently. During full throttle operation the vacuum advance is always at zero (that is, no advance) and the centrifugal system determines the spark setting.

Several different model distributors have been used on the VW engine. The earlier models have 35° centrifugal advance which is adequate for the 5000 rpm range. Later models have a 25° advance and may be modified to give the required 35°.

Year	Distributor type	Centrifugal Advance	Vacuum Advance
1953 & earlier	VE 4 BRS 383	35°	none
1954 & later	VJU 4 BR 3 mk	35°	12°
1954 & later	VJU 4 BR 8 mk	25°	10°

TABLE V

IGNITION

Modify the VJU 4 BR 8 mk by drilling the stop hole for the movable weights from its present size of .266 inches to .312 inches or 5/16 in.

Ideally, of course, the engine should be dynamometer-tested and the weights and springs in the centrifugal advance adjusted for maximum power all through the speed range.

Distributor timing is done with the engine *not* running. Follow the instruction manual and rig a small light in the breaker point circuit. An alternate method is to use a regular neon timing light connected to the coil high tension lead. The small DC light in the point circuit will go out, and the neon bulb will flash when the points "break."

Stock VWs should fire when the notch on the fan pulley is lined up with the joint in the crankcase. Engines built prior to 1954 have this notch located 5° before top dead center (TDC), and engines after 1954 have the notch at 7.5° before TDC. Keeping in mind that 10° is equal to .48 inches along the rim of the pulley it is helpful to mark the TDC, 5°, and 10° before TDC positions. Remember that the pulley rotates clockwise when facing the engine from the rear of the car and that 10° before top dead center (TDC) lines up with the joint before the TDC position.

With 7.5 to 1 compression ratio, timing should be about 5° before TDC, using 85 to 90 octane regular gas. The same setting will operate well with 8.5 to 1 and 95 to 100 octane premium fuel. The best setting produces just a trace of pinging under full throttle in fourth gear at 25 to 35 mph. By all means *experiment* and determine your own best setting.

Coils used on the stock VWs are the Bosch TE6A3 and TE6B1. These may be used on engines up to 7.5 to 1 compression ratio but above that the Bosch TK6A5 Super coil should be used. High compression ratios are more demanding upon the spark source and the extra voltage of the TK6A5 is required.

Bosch and Champion spark plugs seem to work best on the VW. Both types are made in a variety of heat ranges. The Bosch W 225 T1, and Champion L 10S, are suitable for 'round-town driving. Hard driving will require a colder plug such as Champion L11 or Bosch W 240 T1. For competition Bosch W 260 T1 plugs are available. Plug gap should be .026 inches.

SECTION TEN
CLUTCH AND FLYWHEEL

Clutch, flywheel, and pressure plate on the VW are good and sturdy and can be "beefed up" easily for souping.

The engine torque that any clutch system will transmit without slipping depends upon the pressure from the pressure plate springs, the area of the clutch facing material, and the friction coefficient of the lining material. The area on the VW is adequate as it is the same as used on MGs and Porsches up to 1500 cc displacement.

The facing material is cork, which seems to work out well for the stock engine and mild souping jobs. Where temperature might build up because of repeated application, such as during racing, asgestos facing serves much better. Whenever the engine is removed "rough-up" the cork facing with a piece of very heavy sandpaper. It tends to glaze and slip with age.

Pressure for the stock passenger car is supplied by a single set of springs in the pressure plate. The commercial vehicles such as the Kombi and Micro bus use dual springs which give a 25 per cent increase in pressure. The Porsche also uses this arrangement and the extra springs can easily be inserted by a clutch specialist for only a few dollars. The springs are available from any VW dealer.

Since the clutch only needs to transmit the peak torque, 25 per cent extra pressure will just about balance any increase in torque that will occur even with a radical engine. It will also cover mild supercharging such as the Judson. Even the stock clutch works fairly well with the Judson for mild street service.

Figure 14 shows a special clutch that is now available for VW owners from the European Motor Products. It is recommended only if you seem to have trouble after the above modifications have been made.

The following "rules of thumb" are presented to guide you:

1. Add additional clutch springs only if you are upping engine displacement by changing bore and stroke.

2. Do not add clutch springs if the engine does not have to be removed from the car for modification.

3. Change lining only if modifying for racing type competition.

The regular clutch throwout bearing is the carbon plate type and should be given the heave ho unless you cannot purchase a

CLUTCH AND FLYWHEEL

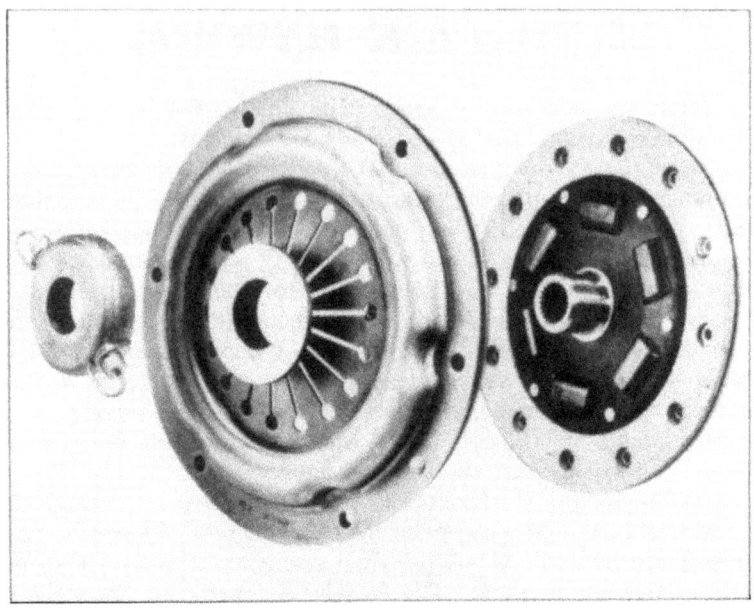

FIGURE 14. Here is a special EMPI 1959 Porsche-type clutch for the Volkswagen.

better type. If possible, replace it with a Porsche or late model VW ball-bearing (including bearing housing). If you use the carbon type with the extra springs excessive drag will just about stall the engine when engaging the clutch at idle.

The VW flywheel is a lucrative place to remove much metal for lightening. Up to five pounds can easily be removed for a 30 per cent reduction in weight. The effect is to reduce the inertia of the rotating parts resulting in a more responsive engine. The biggest improvement occurs if the car accelerates quite rapidly, and then only in the first and second gear. If your planned modifications will reduce your 0 to 60 time below 20 seconds, then flywheel chopping is recommended; if above 20 seconds, improvement will be negligible.

Cut back the side of the flywheel to within ⅛ inch of the pressure plate bolts, leaving *uncut* the part directly below the starter teeth. Always use the type of flywheel nut that correctly fits the transmission shaft. The later model ball and needle bearing nuts do not fit the early transmission shafts.

SECTION ELEVEN

COOLING

The cooling fan on the VW is belt-driven from the crankshaft at approximately two times the crankshaft speed. The fan has more than ample capacity for the stock VW. On the VW a thermostatically-controlled throttle valve located at the fan inlet adjusts engine operating temperature in the same manner as the thermostat in a water-cooled engine. This is necessary so that long down-grades such as are encountered in cold Alpine countries do not cool the engine excessively. It also helps in warming up the engine during cold weather. The fan has such an over-capacity that a common complaint in cold countries is that the VW heater, which diverts the air to the passenger compartment after it leaves the engine, puts out nothing but cold air.

When souping the engine the problem naturally arises as to whether the fan will be able to cool the engine properly. Fortunately someone has tread before us with the Porsche and Denzel, both using the same fan on engines up to 95 horsepower. Porsche and Denzel of course have more cooling fin area than the VW and Okrasa set-ups, but we can probably go to around 75 horsepower without increasing the fin area.

By going to high revs to pick up our horsepower with an unsupercharged engine we can take advantage of the greater cooling capacity at higher fan speds. Supercharged engines pump through considerably more mixture and products of combustion at the same fan speed, thus placing a considerable thermal load on the cooling system.

When we go to the 5000 to 5500 rpm range we must drive the fan at a slower speed than the stock 2 to 1 ratio. A very simple way that works out satisfactorily is to use the slightly longer fan belt for the 1954 Porsche and let it ride farther out on the fan-generator pulley. Fortunately, due to the method of adjustment on the generator pulley, this is possible. The net effect is to increase the size of the fan-generator pulley driving it at a slower speed. This can only be done on the 1954 and later pulleys but they are interchangeable on the crankshaft with the earlier models, and like all VW parts, come at a very reasonable price. The generator pulley will have to be changed also, because the later model belt is a different size.

The following table summarizes the belt sizes:

COOLING

Make & Year	length		width		Angle	Gates number
	in.	mm.	in.	mm.		
VW 1947-1953 & Porsche 1951-1953	35⅜	910	17/32	13.5	40°	8026T
VW 1954-1958	35⅝	905	⅜	9.5	38°	8217
Porsche 1954	36¼	920	⅜	9.5	38°	8226
Porsche 1955-1956	33⅛	840	⅜	9.5	38°	8244

TABLE VI

The belt trick can even be used on stock VWs. Your stocker will make appreciably less noise and give a noticeable increase in power just by installing a slightly longer Porsche belt. Not for blower jobs, however.

Later model Porsches also use a smaller crankshaft pulley to lower the fan speed. These fit on the VW crankshaft but the seal to the case is different. Be sure you check any Porsche pulley to see if it will work before you purchase it.

Clue number two. Keep your spark plug rubbers in good shape or a lot of good cooling air will leak out. They are ridiculously cheap and should always be replaced with a major tune-up, or when obviously not performing their job.

SECTION TWELVE
ENGINE PERFORMANCE

In this section we will discuss what you can expect in power output with different modifications. Although the best approach would be actual dynamometer tests of every change or modification, one at a time, this is impractical because of the amount of money and time required. Instead we will present those combinations of modifications that are popular and readily available, or particularly interesting.

Fortunately, Dr. Porsche did much of this work himself when souping the VW engine to be used in the Porsche automobile. Thus we already have a guide to the amount of power we can expect from the basic design.

Wolfgang Denzel is another name to look up to in the VW souping field. Denzel has surpassed Porsche in obtaining maximum power out of the VW "block". Super versions of the Denzel claim 65 and 85 DIN horsepower for the 1300 cc and 1500 cc sports cars, compared with the latest VW output of 30 DIN horsepower.

Figures 15 and 16 show ten different steps in modifying for more power. Many more combinations of course are possible but these cover the power range nicely and are either well proven or perfectly feasible. Only one plan utilizes supercharging. Although good reliable superchargers are available it is significant that of the experts we have mentioned none selected the supercharger for the VW engine as the way to more power.

The Judson is about the best supercharger for the VW today as it is both reasonably priced and well engineered. Others come and go year by year but Judson is always available for parts and service. The unit is a vane type that gives a six psi boost to the manifold pressure thus boosting more weight flow of air through the engine with a resultant increase in power. Even though it is a positive displacement type it is characteristic of the design to have a rising pressure curve so that the maximum boost pressure is not reached until about 80 per cent of peaking speed.

The Judson supercharger is a simple piece of bolt-on equipment for the VW and represents the largest power increase you can get for your dollar, for just about any automobile built today. It is certainly the best buy if you want the maximum amount of power available, and you are operating on a budget limit around $150.

ENGINE PERFORMANCE

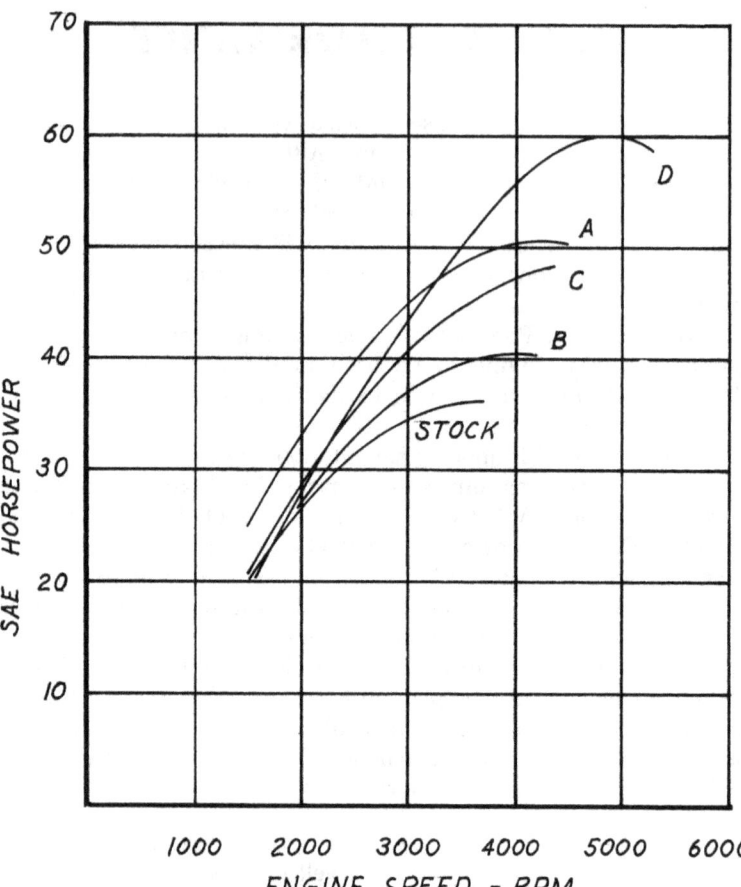

FIGURE 15. This chart depicts the changes which may be expected from increasing the compression ratio in the stock Volkswagen engine

Curve	Description	Comp. ratio	Carburetion	Cam
A	Judson supercharger	6.6	1-28 mm	stock
B	Dual carburetors	6.6	2-28 mm	stock
C	Okrasa	7.5	2-32 mm	stock
D	Okrasa Super	8.5	2-32 mm	super

ENGINE PERFORMANCE

One peculiar advantage of supercharging the VW is that it allows you to obtain the maximum increase in power without digging into the expensive bottom end. As we know the stock VW crank is the major weakness in obtaining more power from the engine. Crank stresses are more a function of speed than any other factor. The added boost that a positive displacement supercharger gives you from 1500 rpm on up means that you do not have to go to the high revs for the extra power. By observing the factory recommended limit of 3400 rpm, with occasional spurts to higher speeds during emergencies, you will probably get through the crank problem without any trouble.

Two other areas of concern must be considered before you invest in a supercharger. The first concerns overheating which is due to the extra "stuff" that you are forcing through the engine whenever under full throttle operation. Although the fan has considerable reserve capacity the higher cylinder and piston temperatures encountered during sustained full throttle operation may lead to piston seizure and ring breakage. Piston clearance recommended by the factory is .0014 to .0022 inches which is rather close for an air-cooled engine. When running temperature is reached the clearance decreases even further, as the aluminum pistons expand more than the cast iron cylinders. The factory, of course, does not know that you are going to supercharge your engine. They have made the clearances as close as possible to eliminate clatter when starting cold, and to allow as much wear as possible for a long life.

The VW fan has enough reserve capacity so that the engine does not overheat to the point of damage and you need not be afraid of piston seizure when supercharging provided you have a clearance of at least .003 to .004 inches when cold. This point probably does not occur naturally until your car has about 20,000 to 30,000 miles on it. A good plan, if you wait to this point, is to install new rings and have the valves ground about 1000 miles prior to installation of the blower. Also include new exhaust valves. While the engine is apart, clean all of the cooling fins so that you will get maximum cooling capacity.

The second serious problem is concerned with combustion chamber deposits induced by the use of leaded gasoline. The higher combustion pressures that are built up with a supercharger necessitate the use of premium gasoline. While regular gas may contain small amounts of tetraethyl lead, premium gas always contains an appreciable amount of it. With the higher head temperatures encountered in air-cooled engines lead from the gas will deposit in the combustion chamber, building up in rough points and sharp

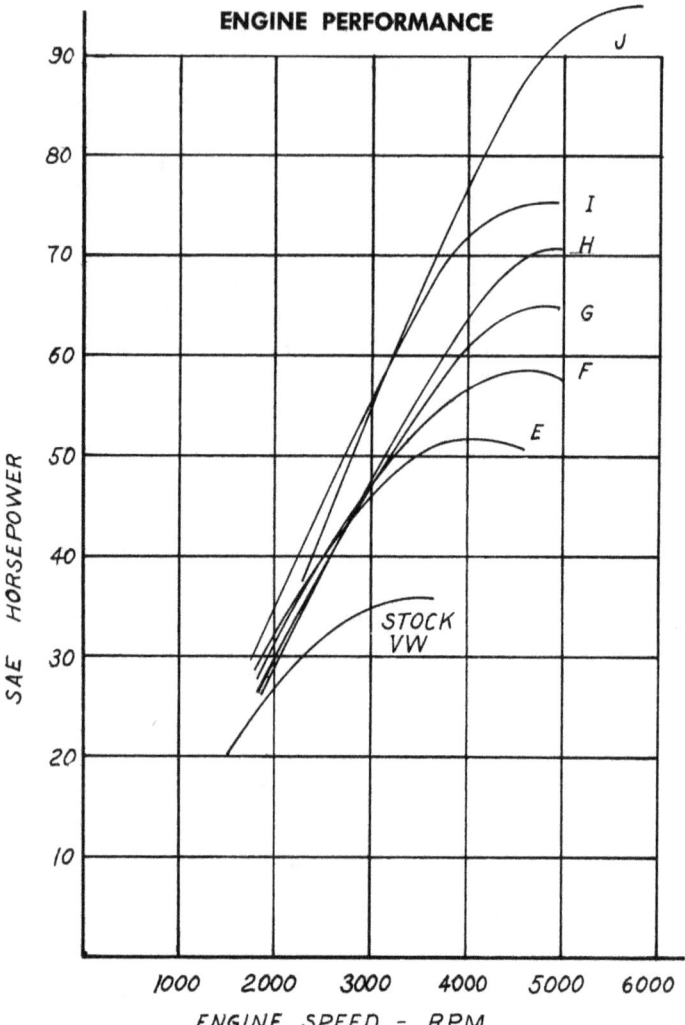

FIGURE 16. This chart depicts the changes which may be expected from changes in bore and stroke of the stock Volkswagen engine. These include the factor of operation at higher top revolution rates.

Curve	Description	Bore mm	Stroke mm	Disp. cc	Comp. ratio	Carburetion	Cam
E	Okrasa 1300	77	69	1285	8.5	2-32-mm	stock
F	Denzel 1300 (kit)	78	67	1281	8.2	2-32 mm	stock
G	Okrasa 1300S	77	69	1285	8.5	2-32 mm	super
H	Denzel 1300S (kit)	78	67	1281	8.2	2-32 mm	super
I	Okrasa-Weber 1500S	79	76.6	1500	8.5	2-40 mm	super
J	Denzel 1500SS	—	—	1500	9.5	2-40 (dual)	wild

ENGINE PERFORMANCE

edges. This is "murder" in any piston engine. The resulting pre-ignition and rough combustion give power a real knockout blow in the solar plexus.

These deposits build up over a certain period of time depending upon the gas and other operating factors but they have become serious in cars with only 10,000 to 20,000 miles under their wheels.

Airlines with air-cooled engines use premium fuel but it is a blend of natural high octane ingredients and contains no tetraethyl lead. Whenever tetraethyl lead is added to aviation gas, spark plug fouling and combustion chamber deposits descend like a plague of locusts.

Of course the deposits are easy to remove and if you are the tinkerer type you may have the heads off every year anyway. You may even be buying a gas that will give you trouble-free service for a much longer time.

Superchargers are a source of several minor irritations that may or may not bother you depending on your own private brand of neuroses. One of these is the oiling system. In order to insure the proper supply of clean oil to the sliding vanes the Judson people have included a separate oiling system. Oil consumption of the separate system varies between one quart per 500 and 1000 miles depending upon how you drive. Since the average VW goes for 1500 to 2000 miles without needing engine oil and naturally needs no water, most owners just forget about the engine compartment entirely and overlook proper oiling of the supercharger.

Noise:—at full power most blowers are not noticeable and the Judson is very commendable in this respect. At idle speed, however, you will swear that there are a few loose screws bouncing around with the vanes. Not loud, but still apparent. If you have overcome the grating on your nerves from the normal whine of a stock VW transmission in fourth at 35 mph then you will not be bothered.

If you are the tinkerer type try a larger carburetor on your Judson. The Ford V-8 60 has been used with success.

Curve A in Figure 15 shows the added power that you may expect with about six pounds of boost pressure such as you get from the Judson.

A point that we should have mentioned earlier is the muffler. One of the first things to do before undertaking any souping is to improve the exhaust system. Either get a good "free breather" as mentioned previously or weld on two larger tail pipes.

All subsequent methods of souping will consider non-supercharged methods of power increase. Free-breathing induction sys-

ENGINE PERFORMANCE

tems, moderate to high speed cams, and boring and stroking will be the route we will follow.

As mentioned previously the BMEP is the most important single fundamental parameter. Figure 16 shows the BMEP plotted for the stock VW, Okrasa, Porsche, and Denzel engines. The problem of the stock VW immediately becomes obvious when all are compared. Although the stock VW has as good BMEP as the other engines when compared on an equal compression ratio basis, the drop-off is extremely rapid at high speed. Our plan will then be to keep the BMEP up, and move the curve to the right as far as possible without sacrificing too much at the lower end.

Free breathing depends on large induction passages with minimum restriction. However, we must be careful of not to use too large carburetors or low speed performance will be extremely poor because of bad fuel-air ratio control and improper atomization.

Table II shows the valve port sizes taken from Iskenderian's chart as a function of different engine sizes at 5000 rpm. This is an arbitrary selection of speed but it represents what will be easy to attain without valve float problems and without overstressing the engine.

The subsequent power curves represent both test data and estimated performance based on similarity factors such as BMEP, valve port sizes, cam timing, carburetor size, displacement, etc. All data are in SAE or gross horsepower units (to make a maximum impression on the fellow occupying the bar stool next to you).

Without altering the breathing an immediate 4 per cent jump in power can be achieved by increasing the compression ratio from 6.6, to 7.5 to 1.

This is about the limit with 85-90 octane regular fuel in an air-cooled engine. Premium 95-100 octane will let you go to 8.5 to 1, but the extra cost starts to cut into the economy angle of the VW.

Don't run right out yet and buy higher compression pistons as this is an uneconomical way to spend your hop-up dollar. Wait until you have to change the pistons for some other reason and then take advantage of the boost in compression ratio. Also, some of the conversion kits will boost the compression ratio by reducing the head volume or increasing the stroke without even changing the pistons.

ENGINE PERFORMANCE

The first improvement in breathing incorporates the use of dual carburetors feeding through short individual manifolds. This is so fundamental that it is used on all subsequent plans. However, it pays off handsomely only in the higher rpm ranges so that not too much can be expected if you are stuck with the factory rev limit of 3400. However, for intermittent use, or if you have a sound bottom end, you can run higher.

Duals will give you up to a 15 per cent increase in power at about 4200 rpm. Starting is greatly improved, idling is still good, and you may find it gives you the little extra kick you want, if you are not power mad. Installation is usually easy, and can be accomplished with only a few tools. Dual carbs may be had for as little as $80. Curve B of Figure 15 illustrates two-carb performance.

Curve C of Figure 15 is the next one of interest. Output is 48 hp at 4200 rpm with the Okrasa dual carb head kit. This is a ·33 per cent increase still using stock bore, stroke, and cam. Compression ratio increase from 6.6 to 7.5 accounts for 4 per cent of the power increase. Money involved is $250, but you are buying a high quality piece of equipment that will last a long time, and may even be modified for better output. Even if you don't do anything to the bottom end you can install the Okrasa heads and drive around town until something pops. Then tear into both the crank and cam. This is like the installment plan with a lot of fun from the beginning.

Figure 15 is intended to show how far you can go with a reliable and smooth running engine with stock bore and stroke. Curve D is about the limit, and we are calling this an Okrasa "Super" since it uses the Okrasa kit with an 8.5 to 1 compression ratio and an Iskenderian 2J camshaft which is very close to the Porsche Super grind. Peak power is a fat 60 horsepower which will amaze your Porsche 1500 America coupe friends and give fits to your MG A enemies. This is a "best buy" in engines. Cam, crank shot-peening, and balancing will run about $85, which puts you in the $330 bracket for parts with a healthy 67 per cent power increase.

If your budget is tight and your car doesn't have over 20,000 miles on it, you can use your old bearings and pistons. If you care to drop 2.5 hp and buy *regular* instead of *premium* gas, then stick with 7.5 to 1 compression ratio.

The next batch of modifications including bore and stroke changes are shown in Figure 16. If you are the squeamish type who are appalled by putting up to 90 horsepower in a VW, then do not look. However, if you are power-mad like we are, then the curves will really look voluptuous.

ENGINE PERFORMANCE

Curve E is first and shows what happens when you use the Okrasa heads and 5 mm stroker crank and the stock VW cam. The crank accounts for an 8 per cent increase over curve C. The crank is $140 which puts you in the $390 outgo bracket. However, once you have the bottom end apart we recommend that you skip this step entirely and jump to curve G, install the 2J cam, and reap another 25 per cent power jump for only $35.

Curve F shows the output of the Denzel kit for the VW. A neat boost of 64 per cent over stock can be had for a rather shocking price of $600. The Denzel kit does give phenomenal value in that it includes new pistons, Porsche-type aluminum cylinders, crank, and Porsche-size heads with big valves and more cooling fin area. By all means do not install this set-up without a super-type cam as the 2J. In other words skip to curve H for a 100 per cent power increase over stock. Now the $600 does not look quite so bad. The Denzel heads are not available separately from the rest of the kit but a lot of people are jumping into the VW market and do not be surprised if individual heads similar to these are available soon. If possible, stick on larger carbs such as the 40 mm Solexes, but in any case use at least 26 mm venturis.

Combining the Okrasa heads with .10 inch larger valves together with Weber ½-inch stroker kit we can now work ourselves up to a brutish 75 horsepower output with a full 1500 cc engine. This is still somewhat a makeshift engine since we do not have the breathing capacity that we would like, but as of this writing no other equipment is made specifically for souping the VW. This engine would cost about $500 for parts alone but would give you fantastic performance.

Curve J shows the probable ultimate that can be wrung out of the basic crankcase. We call this one a Denzel 1500 "Super Super." The cam will probably be some wild grind that has a lumpy idle and won't come in until about 3500 rpm but you could sure bring the trophies home. Curve J indicates about one hp per cubic inch which is about all there is in any push-rod engine.

All the conversions will give you equal, or better, gasoline mileage than the stock VW—that is, 30 to 35 mpg, for the same stock VW performance. However, if you take advantage of the extra power continuously you should expect a drop of two to five miles per gallon.

SECTION THIRTEEN
TUNE-UP INSTRUCTIONS

For the first 1000 to 2000 miles after installing a new engine in your VW do not drive at full power except for short spurts. Important hazards to avoid in a new engine are excessive speed and overheating. After the first 500 miles, open the engine up to top speed and power frequently, but do not hold these conditions for more than 5 to 10 seconds at a time. Remember that the fan cools best when run between 3000 and 4000 rpm engine speed. *Avoid lugging below 2000 rpm.*

If you are using Solex carburetors you have a wide variety of jet sizes and air venturi sizes available, so that you can satisfy any condition that you want. The Solex carburetor is a fixed venturi type with accelerator pump similar to the ones used on American cars. It has one advantage over most American carburetors in that the venturi and all jets may be readily changed.

The stock VW carb, 28 PCI, is used on the VW only and is supplied with a 21.5 mm venturi. It is the only Solex model that uses a butterfly valve for choking when starting cold. All other Solexes with choke have a separate tiny, carburetor within a carburetor, air and fuel enrichening system which by-passes the main throttle butterfly when activated for cold starting. The first numbers in the model designation indicate the diameter of the main air passage at the throttle butterfly. Thus the 28 PCI has a 28 mm throttle and the 32 PBI has a 32 mm throttle, etc.

The 32 PBIC with choke is the most common model and is used on a wide variety of cars from Borgwards to Volvos. The 40 PBIC, used on Porsche Supers is just like the 32 PBIC except for its size. The 40 PII is a double-barreled job used on the Spyder engine.

Other carburetors such as the old Ford V-8 60 have been used successfully on hoppd-up VWs but the Solex parts are the most convenient to obtain as they are used on many imported cars. Also if you have your work done, at a regular VW-Porsche dealer, gaskets and other parts will be readily available.

The following table summarizes jets for the VW, Okrasa, and Porsches. Porsche data are included so that you may judge what to do if you go beyond the stock Okrasa.

TUNE-UP INSTRUCTIONS

Item	VW 1192	Okrasa 1192	Okrasa 1300	Porsche 1300	Porsche 1500	Porsche 1500S	
Model	1954			356	546	527	528
Carb size mm	28	32	32	32	32	32	40
Main jet	122.5	112.5	115	115	120	120	117.5(135)°
Air Correction jet	200	240	240	240	260	180	160
Venturi mm	21.5	23	24	24	24	26	26 (29)°
Idle fuel jet	50	50	50	60	55	55	55
Idle air bleed	0.8	1.0	1.0	1.0	1.0	1.0	2.2
Emulsion tube	29	23	23	23	28	23	23
Float weight gr.	12.5	12.5	12.5	12.5	12.5	12.5	21
Accelerator jet	50	45	45	55	55	55	60
Idle needle valve	1.5	1.5	1.5	1.5	2.0	1.5	2.0
Start (choke) fuel		120	120	120	120	120	120
Start (choke) air		3.5	3.5	3.5	3.5	3.5	3.5
Accelerator Pump		0.5 cc per stroke all					

(°) Competition or sport size

TABLE VII

For an individual engine installation the above sizes may be varied a size or two one way or the other depending upon your own road tests. Enlarging the main jet richens the power mixture under the full range of full throttle operation. Enlarging the air correction jet leans out the mixture at high rpms.

A good way to check your mixture ratio is to observe the color of the inside of your exhaust pipes. If they are dark and sooty the engine is running rich and is wasting gas. If they are an extremely light grey the engine is running too lean and can be damaged by overheating. The correct color is in the range of a reddish dark brown to a dark grey.

Dual carburetors must be synchronized so that both are all the way open at full throttle, and meter the same amount of air and fuel during idle. The most critical setting is at idle, and if you have this set properly it is very simple to check the open position.

The important point is to have both carburetors admitting the same amount of fuel and air to each bank of cylinders at idle speed. The best way to set the air flow is with an actual air metering device such as an Air Syn or Uni Syn. These are both actually small air flow meters that can be temporarily mounted at the inlet

TUNE-UP INSTRUCTIONS

of a carburetor to accurately measure the flow of air into the cylinders. The butterfly position determines the flow of air. The linkage to the carburetors should be disconnected, and each carburetor should be adjusted independently until both are equal, with the engine at operating temperature.

Next, the idle mixture ratio should be adjusted at each carburetor until a point is found, between lean and rich, at which the engine runs smoothly and close to its maximum speed for the idle butterfly setting. Readjust idle speed and mixture ratio until you are satisfied. Reconnect carburetor linkage keeping same relative throttle positions to retain synchronization. In some cases this requires the fabrication of a special adjusting block for exact synchronization. Saw the throttle linkage in two between the carburetors and insert the ends in a small block with a set-screw for each side.

When changing venturis remember that larger venturis mean less pressure drop for drawing the fuel through the fuel metering jets, thus larger fuel jets are required. The main jet and the air correction jet are usually the only ones requiring changing.

Large venturis give maximum power at top rpm but contribute to poor engine response at full throttle and low rpm. Rich mixtures are required for maximum power. Lean mixtures give the best gasoline mileage. Too lean mixtures are particularly harmful in an air-cooled engine resulting in piston seizure, excessive pinging, and valve burning.

Tune-up procedure is the same as for other cars and is presented in the following outline:

1. Adjust valve tappets when cold to manufacturer's specifications.
2. Clean and adjust spark plugs to .026" gap.
3. Adjust distributor points to .016" gap.
4. Set distributor timing, with engine stopped, to fire 5° to 7° before top dead center.
5. Start engine and set dual carburetors.
6. Road test and set fan throttle position to .75 to 1.0 inch opening after hard driving.
7. Stop engine and check all miscellaneous items such as gas lines, fan belt, oil filter, bolts, and nuts.
8. After 100 miles check exhaust color for correct carburetor jets.

SECTION FOURTEEN
TECHNICAL DATA AND STATISTICS

This section contains technical data that will be useful for modifying the VW. Okrasa, Porsche and Denzel data are also shown for comparison.

Item		VW 1954 and later	VW with Okrasa heads	VW with Denzel heads	Porsche 1500 America	Porsche 1500 Super	Denzel 1300 Super
Bore	mm.	77	77	78	80	80	78
	in.	3.030	3.030				
Stroke	mm.	64	64	67	74	74	67
	in	2.52	2.52				
Displ.	cc	1192	1192	1281	1488	1488	1281
	cu. in.	72.7	72.7	78.1	90.7	90.7	78.1
Compr. Ratio		6.6	7.5	8.2	7.5	8.5	8.5
Intake Valve	mm.	30	33	38	38	38	38*
	in.	1.18	1.30	1.50	1.50	1.50	1.50*
Exhaust Valve	mm.	28	28	32	31	31	32*
	in.	1.10	1.10	1.26	1.22	1.22	1.26*
Intake Port	mm.	25	28	33*	33	33	33*
	in.	.99	1.10	1.30*	1.30	1.30	1.30*
Exhaust Port	mm.	24	24	27*	26	26	27*
	in.	.95	.95	1.07*	1.03	1.03	1.07*
Camshaft							
Int. open		2.5°	2.5°	2.5°	2.5°	19°	19°*
Int. close		37.5°	37.5°	37.5°	37.5°	54°	54°*
Exh. open		37.5°	37.5°	37.5°	37.5°	54°	54°*
Exh. close		2.5°	2.5°	2.5°	2.5°	19°	19°*
Carburetor No. Used		1	2	2	2	2	2 dual
Throttle size	mm.	28	32	32	32	40	40
	in.	1.10	1.26	1.26	1.26	1.58	1.58
Venturi size	mm.	21.5	23	23*	24	26	24*
	in.	.85	.91	.91*	.95	1.03	.95*
Horsepower	DIN	30@3700	41@4200	50*@4500	55@4500	70@5000	65@5400
	SAE	36@3700	48@4200	59*@4500	65@4500	83@5000	76@5400
Torque lb./ft.	DIN	58@1900	63@2200	70*@2700	79@2700	82@3700	71@4400
	SAE	68@1900	75@2200	83*@2700	93@2700	97@3700	83@4400
HP per cu. in	DIN	.41	.56	.64	.61	.77	.83
	SAE	.50	.66	.76	.72	.91	.97

*estimated

**TABLE VIII
SPECIFICATION DATA**

Weight data (stock VW)

Crankcase & studs	35.0
Crankshaft	14.0
Flywheel	17.3
Pressure Plate	5.5
Clutch	1.3
Pulley	1.7
Camshaft and Gear	2.7
Connecting Rods (4)	3.0
Cylinders (4)	14.0
Pistons, Pins & Rings (4)	4.0
Cylinder Heads (2)	16.6
Fan & Generator	15.0
Carburetor	2.5
Coil	2.0
Distributor	3.0
Sheet Metal, Nuts, & Misc.	14.0
Total (engine)	151.6
Exhaust System (Muffler)	11.5
Total (complete)	163.1

TABLE IX

Band leader, Louis Prima, with his idea of hopping up the Volkswagen.

FIGURE 17. Here is a Judson supercharger installation in a Volkswagen sedan. The air cleaner cannot be used in Karmann-Ghia and Transporter series.

85

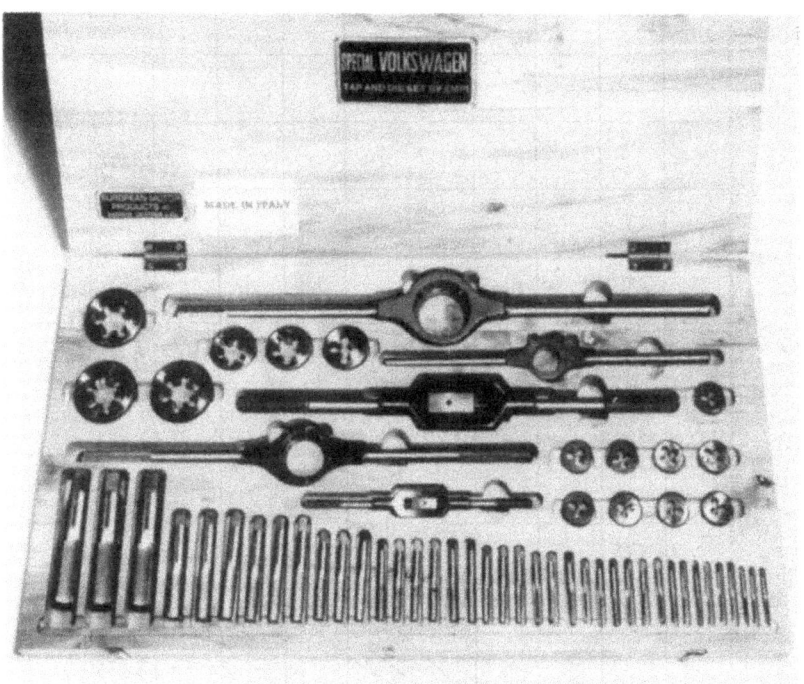

FIGURE 18. These metric-unit taps and dies are available from the Italian maker as a complete set, as shown, or the individual units may be bought separately.

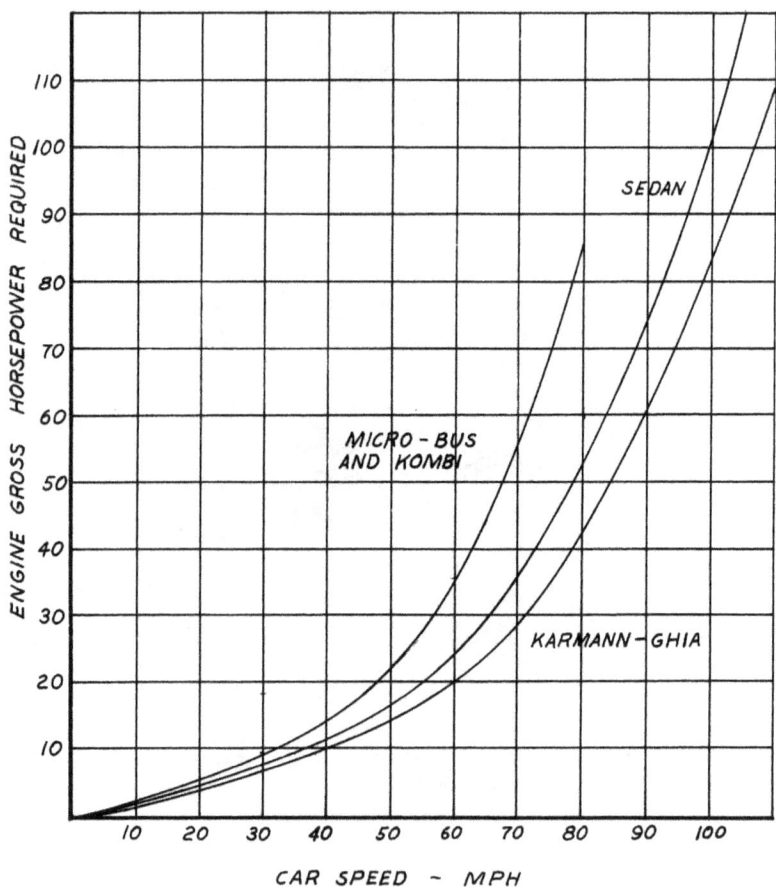

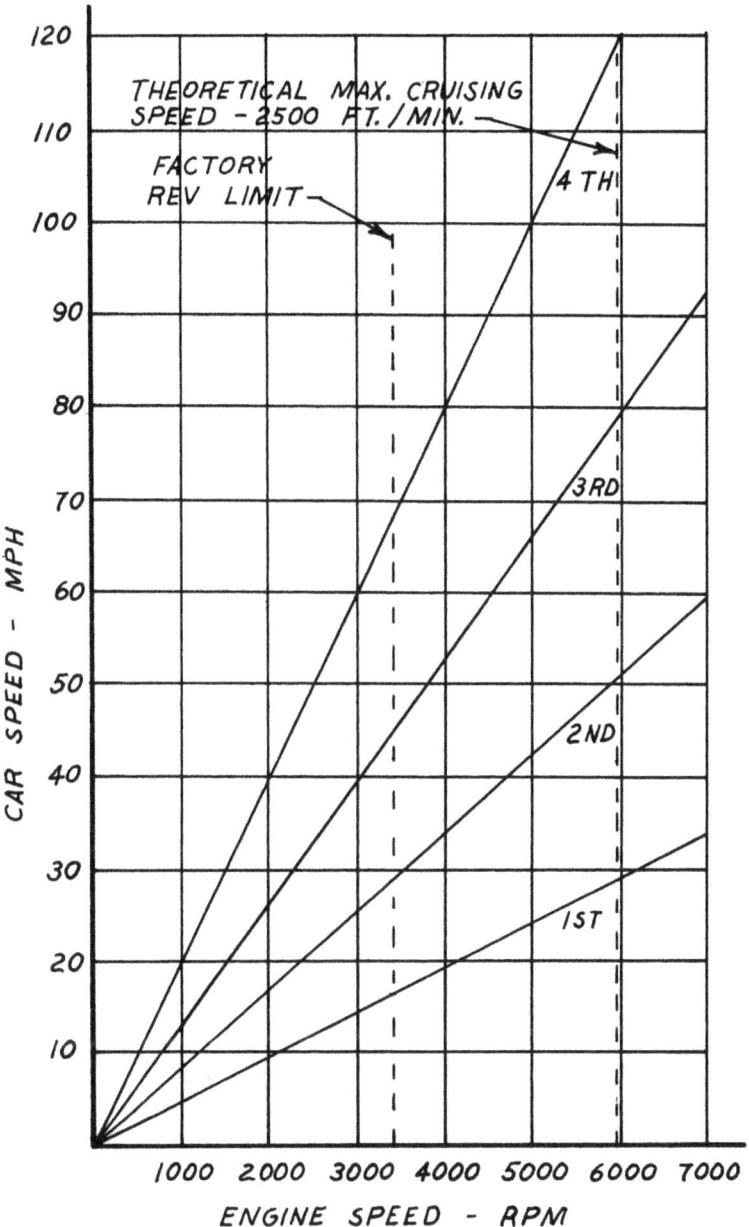

FIGURE 19. This Weber stroker kit includes a cast billet crank, stroker pistons and a reground camshaft.

Stan Mott

The cross-country "cheapskate" free-loader.

FIGURE 20. Frank Atkinson and his trophy-winning Volkswagen. Note that the rear wheels have a wider tread than those in front.

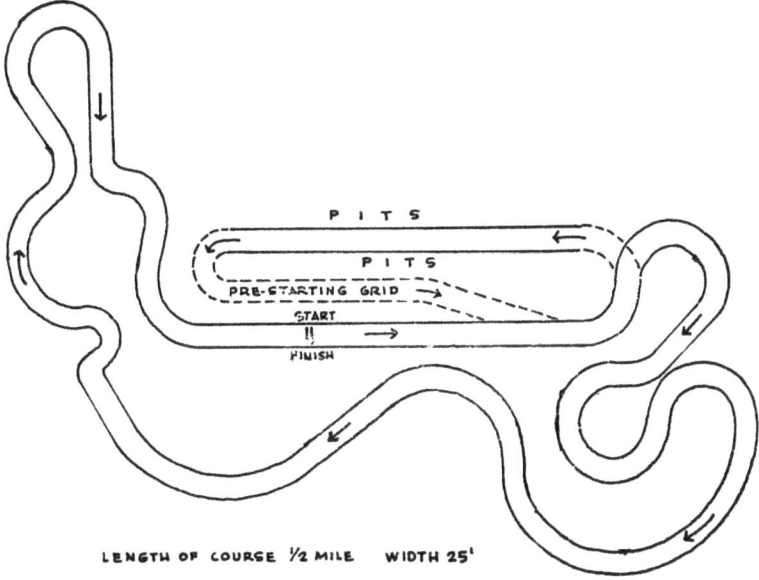

Drawing of the course on which Frank Atkinson of San Gabriel, California, "knocked 'em over" with his modified VW convertible on July 13, 1958.

An as example of what you can do with a Volkswagen let's turn the spotlight on Frank Atkinson of San Gabriel, Calif. An experienced driver of time trials and slaloms, Frank turned in the following amazing performance in a mildly modified 1300 cc heavy VW convertible, competing in the Singer Owners' Club "Time-Tralom" during July 1958. Out of a field of 194 entries on the race track-type course he:

Beat all Triumph TR-2s and TR-3s (14 entered).
Beat all Morgans (6).
Beat all but two Austin-Healeys (13).
Beat all but two MGs (18).
Beat all but two Corvettes (6).
Beat all but two Jaguars (6).
Beat two-thirds of all Porsches (16).
Beat all but two cars in Class G (1300 cc).
Beat all cars in Class E (1600-2000 cc).
Beat all but two cars in Class F (2000-2700 cc).
Beat all sedans by at least two seconds (1600 cc).
Beat best stock VW by four seconds.
Was only 1.84 seconds behind fastest time of the day, 1:08.82.

Frank finds that the sway bar in front, decambered rear wheels, Englebert Competition P tires in front and Michelin X in the rear bring the VW right up to sports car handling standards. He won six slalom trophies before the S.O.C. Tralom against sports cars, not sedans, and in one case was beaten only by a Denzel 1300 for fastest time of the day.

His convertible has Okrasa heads and 5 mm stroker crank, Isky 2J cam and Kombi clutch. Rods and crank shot-peened and all major parts balanced.

FIGURE 21. Both miles per hour and engine revs may be read from "Ecotac", produced by Advanced Car Specialties of Toronto, fitting outside the speedometer glass of all VW cars except Karmann-Ghia. For each gear it shows engine speeds, VW-recommended minimum and maximum revs, and peak torque and horsepower points.

FIGURE 22. Typical instruments that will enhance your driving pleasure in the Volkswagen are shown above from Fisher Products. This Motometer Three-In-One Dashboard ensemble includes fuel level gauge, oil temperature gauge and precision ammeter.

The following pages actually have nothing to do with "Souping the Volkswagen" but they do give important and interesting information on the standard model VW. —Clymer.

CARBURETOR TROUBLE CHECKING

SYMPTOM   **CAUSE**   **REMEDY**

1. Engine will not start (with fuel in tank, ignition in order, and choke closed)
   - a. Choke does not fully close
   - a. Eliminate jamming, replace choke if necessary. Do not overtighten air cleaner clamping screw
   - b. Choke poppet valve sticks or does not fully close
   - b. Repair or replace choke poppet valve
   - c. No fuel in system
   - c. Check in the following order: Release main jet carrier. If fuel is coming out, the main jet is obstructed. If no fuel is coming out, disconnect pipe to fuel pump and set starter in motion without turning the ignition key. If there is a well-defined spurt of fuel at every working stroke of the pump, the float needle valve is clogged up. If not fuel is ejected, it may be due to: pump valves sticking, pump mechanism at fault, dirt in fuel shut-off cock

2. Flat spot at idling speed
   - a. Pilot jet blocked up
   - a. Clean pilot jet
   - b. Induction air leakage at flange. Cracks in induction manifold
   - b. Tighten induction manifold flanges, replace gaskets if necessary. Check induction manifold for air leakage. Weld or renew cracked induction manifolds.
   - c. Volume control screw damaged (tip broken off)
   - c. Replace volume control screw (remove tip, if broken off)
   - d. Idling mixture too lean
   - d. Properly adjust idle mixture and idle speed so that engine runs evenly and steadily

3. Poor acceleration
   - a. Idling mixture too lean
   - a. Properly adjust idle mixture and idle speed so that engine runs evenly and steadily
   - b. Accelerator pump diaphragm leaky
   - b. Check and, if necessary, replace diaphragm

4. Engine stalls when suddenly releasing accelerator pedal
   - Idle mixture too rich
   - Check and correct idle adjustment

5. Engine runs uneven at low idle speed and exhaust soots excessively at high idle speed
   Spark plugs tend to soot up and fail to produce sparks
   - a. Excess pressure on float needle valve
   - a. Check pump pressure, reduce if necessary
   - b. Float leaky
   - b. Replace float
   - c. Float needle valve does not close
   - c. Clean or replace float needle valve

6. Engine runs uneven, misfires, and cuts out at full throttle
   Fuel starvation
   - a. Clean main jet
   - b. Clean float needle valve
   - c. Check pump pressure, increase if necessary
   - d. Clean fuel shut-off cock

7. Excess fuel consumption
   - a. Jet sizes not properly adapted to one another
   - a. Install correct set of jets. Check "face" of spark plugs
   - b. Excess pressure on float needle valve
   - b. Check pump pressure reduce if necessary
   - c. Float leaky
   - c. Replace float
   - d. Float needle valve does not close
   - d. Check float needle valve and replace if necessary

Note: Poor acceleration and a tendency of the engine to stall when idling may also be due to an insufficiently advanced ignition, too low a breaker point gap, or dirty spark plugs. Always check ignition system when in doubt.

FUEL PUMP TROUBLE CHECKING

SYMPTOM / CAUSE	REMEDY
1. *Pump leaky at jointing faces: Loss of fuel*	
a. Slotted screws insecure	a. Tighten screws
b. Diaphragm cracked	b. Renew diaphragm (VW 328 b)
2. *Diaphragm leaks at rivets: Loss of fuel*	
Diaphragm damaged by unskilled assembly	Renew diaphragm (VW 328 b)
3. *Diaphragm material leaky: Loss of fuel*	
Diaphragm material damaged by solvent substance in fuel	Renew diaphragm (VW 328 b)
4. *Excessive pump stroke: Overstraining the diaphragm*	
Pump incorrectly installed, gasket too thin	Correctly install pump (VW 328 a), check diaphragm, if necessary
5. *Pump pressure low*	
a. Pump incorrectly installed, gasket too thin	a. Correctly install pump (VW 328 a)
b. Spring pressure low	b. Renew spring or, if necessary, stretch it apart
6. *Pump pressure excessive: Float needle valve forced down*	
a. Pump incorrectly installed, gasket too thin	a. Correctly install pump (VW 328 a)
b. Spring pressure excessive	b. Renew spring or, if necessary, bring intermediate turns further together
7. *Fuel pump inoperative or insufficient fuel delivery*	
Valves leaky or sticking	Check valves, renew valves and valve seats, if necessary

GENERATOR TROUBLE CHECKING

SYMPTOM / CAUSE	REMEDY
Generator lamp does not light with ignition switched on	
a. Battery discharged	a. Charge battery
b. Battery defective	b. Renew battery
c. Bulb burned out	c. Renew bulb
d. Corroded or loose battery terminals	d. Clean or tighten terminals respectively
e. Loose connections or broken cables	e. Tighten or repair cables respectively
f. Ignition switch defective	f. Renew ignition switch
g. Generator brushes do not make contact with commutator	g. Make the brushes to move freely or renew brushes. If necessary, renew the brush springs
Generator lamp does not go out or flares up when engine is accelerated	
a. Drive belt loose or faulty	a. Adjust belt tension or renew belt
b. Regulator faulty	b. Renew regulator
c. Charging cables loose or disrupted	c. Check cables and connections
d. Generator faulty	d. Check generator
Generator lamp goes out only at high speed	
a. Generator faulty	a. Check generator
b. Regulator faulty	b. Renew regulator
Generator lamp continues to light with the ignition switched off	
a. Regulator contact points sticking (burned)	a. Renew regulator

STARTING MOTOR TROUBLE CHECKING

SYMPTOM / CAUSE	REMEDY

Starter does not operate when pressing button
Switch on the lamps when testing:
- a. Lights do not burn. Loose cables or poor ground connection. Battery run down
- b. Lights go out when pressing starter button. Insufficient current due to loose connections or corroded terminals
- c. Lights go dim when pressing starter button. Battery run down
- d. Lights stay bright when pressing starter button. Make a jumper contact between terminals 30 and 50 at starting motor: If the starting motor operates, there is an open circuit in cable 50 to starter button, or in cable 30 to lighting switch, or the starter button is defective
- e. Lights stay bright and plunger in solenoid switch is pulled when pressing starter button. Disconnect battery cable from terminal 30 at starting motor and connect it to terminal stud of connector (contact blade). If the starting motor operates, the contacts of the solenoid switch are worn or dirty

Remedy:
- a. Check battery cables and connection. Test voltage of battery
- b. Clean battery terminals and cable clamps, clean and tighten connections between battery, starting motor and ground
- c. Charge battery
- d. Eliminate open circuits, replace defective parts
- e. Replace solenoid switch

Starting motor does not operate when battery cable is directly connected with terminal stud of connector (contact) blade
- a. Brushes sticking
- b. Brushes worn
- c. Weak spring tension. Brushes do not make contact
- d. Commutator dirty
- e. Commutator rough, pitted, or burned
- f. Armature or field coils defective

Remedy:
- a. Clean brushes and guides of brush holders
- b. Replace brushes
- c. Replace springs
- d. Clean commutator
- e. Recondition starting motor
- f. Overhaul starting motor

Sluggish or slow action of the starting motor
- a. Battery run down
- b. Insufficient current flow due to loose or corroded connections
- c. Brushes sticking
- d. Brushes worn
- e. Commutator dirty
- f. Commutator rough, pitted, or burned
- g. Armature or field coils defective

Remedy:
- a. Charge battery
- b. Clean battery terminals and cable clamps, tighten connections
- c. Clean brushes and guides of brush holders
- d. Replace brushes
- e. Clean commutator
- f. Recondition starting motor
- g. Overhaul starting motor

Starting motor is heard to operate, but cranks engine erratically or not at all
- a. Drive pinion defective
- b. Flywheel gear ring defective

Remedy:
- a. Replace drive pinion
- b. Replace flywheel or remachine gear ring

Drive pinion does not move out of mesh
- a. Drive pinion armature shaft dirty or damaged
- b. Solenoid switch defective

Remedy:
- a. Overhaul starting motor
- b. Replace solenoid switch

CLUTCH TROUBLE CHECKING

SYMPTOM / CAUSE	REMEDY
1. Noise	
a. Pilot bush in flywheel gland nut worn	a. Renew bush and fill in with 10 gr. Universal Grease VW — A 052
b. Carbon thrust ring excessively worn	b. Renew carbon thrust ring. See to it that release plate and clutch clearance are correctly adjusted. Tell driver not to use clutch pedal as a foot rest
c. Driven plate fouling pressure plate	c. Renew or straighten driven plate
d. Weak release lever springs or unequal tension	d. Renew springs
2. Chatter or Grabbing	
a. Transmission case not tightly mounted	a. Tighten mounting bolts and nuts
b. Bend of cable guide tube not correct	b. Correct the bend to 10 or 20 mm (.4" or 8")
c. Grease or oil on driven plate, flywheel or pressure plate	c. Renew oil seal. Clean all parts and reline driven plate
d. Uneven contact of pressure plate	d. Renew or regrind pressure plate
e. Release plate not running true	e. Eliminate run-out. Max. permissible run-out: 0.3 mm (0.012")
f. Unequal tension of thrust springs	f. Renew thrust springs
3. Dragging or Incomplete Release	
a. Excessive pedal free play	a. Adjust clutch clearance: 10 - 20 mm (0.4" - 0.8") at clutch pedal
b. Distorted driven plate or bent main drive shaft	b. Straighten or renew driven plate or main drive shaft
c. Cushion segments excessively set or plate linings broken	c. Reline or replace driven plate
4. Slippage	
a. Lack of pedal free play due to wear of linings	a. Adjust clutch clearance: 10 - 20 mm (0.4" - 0.8") at clutch pedal
b. Grease or oil on clutch linings	b. Replace clutch linings. Replace engine or transmission oil seal if necessary

LUBRICATION — FRONT AXLE

IMPORTANT—A perfect lubrication of the front axle bearing points is only insured with the front axle raised off its wheels (unloaded condition). Grease should be injected into the nipples until the excess grease begins to emerge at the edges of the lubrication points. The service life of the front axle depends on skilled lubrication with trade-mark lubricants which correspond with the specifications given by the Volkswagenwerk. When lubricating, the grease nipples and grease guns should be perfectly clean.

STEERING TROUBLE CHECKING

SYMPTOM **CAUSE** **REMEDY**

HARD STEERING. Steering is equally stiff from lock to lock, jams or front wheels do not automatically resume straight-ahead position after a turn.

a. Front axle inadequately lubricated

b. King pins stiff or seized

c. Steering gear maladjusted

d. Steering sector not matching the steering worm, i.e., the sector does not bear on the root when new, but on the flanks only, allowing it to tilt during operation

e. Ball-shaped surface of sector or concave recess in sector shaft damaged

f. Sector shaft seized up in bore of steering gear case

g. The spring pressure on the sector shaft is too high: Sector shaft end play improperly adjusted, steering sector too large, thrust spring too long or in too much tension. Length of thrust pin: 20.1/19.9 mm (.79"/.75"). Free length of thrust pin: 23.8/23.0 mm (.94"/.91"). Length and load of installed spring: 60 - 75 kg (132 - 165 lbs.) 20.3 mm (.91")

h. Steering worm thrust bearing cups damaged, restricting the movement of the balls

a. Jack up front end of car and thoroughly lubricate front axle

b. Jack up car and disconnect tie rods. Try to make stiff king pins move freely by thoroughly lubricating them (if necessary with thin oil). If seized, remove king pin and exchange damaged components.

c. Check steering gear adjustments. Adjust sector shaft and worm shaft end play as prescribed. If necessary, exchange steering set (sector shaft, sector, and worm). Check oil level.

d. Check impression of contact between steering worm and sector, if necessary replace steering gear set (worm, sector, and sector shaft). In less severe cases, a remedy may be effected by carefully lapping the sector to the worm. To do this, clamp the worm in the chuck of a lathe and use fine grinding compound. Prior to re-assembly, remove all traces of the grinding compound and recheck impression of contact

e. Renew steering gear set. Check impression of contact before final assembly

f. If only slight signs of seizure evident, these should be carefully removed and the shaft polished. Permissible clearance between shaft and bore: 0.040 - 0.082 mm (.0016" - .0032")

g. Check parts and replace as found necessary. The spring may be ground off so that its end is only 0.9 - 1.5 mm (.35" - 0.59") above the thrust pin face in the unloaded condition

h. Check thrust bearings for free movement, replace if necessary. Care should be exercised when pressing the end cover and the upper thrust bearing into the steering gear case. Sealing compound should not enter the lower thrust bearing. The outer edge of the upper thrust bearing cup should be free from burrs in the wall of the bore when pressing the cup in position. Such metal clips would enter the lower thrust bearing

Hard steering and squeaking noise

    a. Steering wheel binding in steering column top bush

        a. Check position of steering column; if necessary, check and correct position of steering gear (check toe-in). Inspect steering column top bush. Lubricate or exchange as necessary.

    b. Steering wheel hub chafing on steering column top bush face

        b. Bush too far projecting from steering column tube or steering column tube positioned too high. Lower the tube

Hard steering, unequal resistance and chafing noise

    Steering column fouling steering column tube

        Alter position of steering gear so that the steering column is correctly centered in the steering column tube (check toe-in)

Front wheels do not resume straight-ahead position after a turn, although there is no binding in the steering system

    a. Front wheels improperly adjusted

        a. Check and adjust front wheel alignment (caster, camber and toe-in)

    b. Steering arms of stub axles (steering knuckles) bent or twisted

        b. Remove stub axles and check them for bends and twisting with the gauge VW 258a. Replace if necessary

EXCESSIVE PLAY IN STEERING SYSTEM

Excessive clearance between steering wheel and steering column top bush

    Bush worn

        Renew bush

Excessive play in steering gear

    a. Steering gear improperly adjusted

        a. Check steering gear adjustments. Adjust sector shaft and worn shaft end play as prescribed

    b. Steering set worn

        b. Exchange steering set (sector shaft, sector, and worm)

Excessive play in tie rod joints

    Ball studs worn

        Exchange worn ball studs

Excessive play in front wheel suspension

    Worn bearing points (torsion arms, torsion arm links, stub axle, and front wheel bearings)

        Check adjustments of torsion arm link pins and front wheel bearings. Renew excessively worn parts

SERVICE DIAGNOSIS OF ABNORMAL TIRE WEAR

TYPE OF WEAR	CAUSE
Wear at the sides of the tread.	Underinflation.
Wear at the center of the tread.	Overinflation.
Spotty or irregular wear (gouges and waves).	Wheel assembly static and dynamic unbalance. Lateral wheel run-out. Excessive play in wheel bearings or at king pin.
Lightly worn spots at the center of the tread (cups).	Wheel and tire static unbalance. Radial wheel run-out.
Flat spots at the center of the tread.	Violent brake application. Brake drum out of round. Check brakes!
Heel and toe wear (saw-tooth effect with one end of each tread block worn more than the other) leading to cracks in the fabric structure which become visible outside in the long run.	Typical for overloading. Check inside of tire casing for cracks.
a. Side wear.	a. Incorrect camber. Continual driving on steeply cambered (high-crowned) roads.
b. Feather edge of rubber on one side of the tread blocks.	b. Wheels toe-in or toe-out excessively. If the rear wheels are concerned, check adjustment of spring plate and effect of shock absorbers.
c. Rounding and roughening of the tread at the outside shoulder of the tire.	c. Caused by high speed driving on curves, called cornering wear.

BRAKE TROUBLE CHECKING

SYMPTOM   **CAUSE**   **REMEDY**

Pedal goes to floorboard
    Normal lining wear   Adjust shoes

Spongy response at brake pedal
    a. Air in the system   a. Bleed the system
    b. Lack of fluid in master cylinder reservoir   b. Top up fluid level

Pedal goes to floorboard without brake action, even though the system has been bled and adjusted
    a. Check valve in master cylinder inoperative   a. Renew the check valve
    b. Check valve seat dirty   b. Clean or renew check valve seat

Brake action is obtained only by pumping pedal several times
    a. Air in the system   a. Bleed the system
    b. Weak piston return spring   b. Renew piston return spring

Brake action decreases and pedal goes to floorboard, even though the brakes have been adjusted
    a. Fluid leak in the system   a. Locate point of leakage and repair
    b. Damaged or unserviceable cups in master   b. Replace faulty cups
        or wheel cylinder

Brakes drag
    a. By-pass port in master cylinder clogged   a. Clean the master cylinder
    b. Too less a clearance between piston push   b. Adjust brake pedal play
        rod and master cylinder piston
    c. Shoe return springs broken or weak   c. Replace springs and adjust shoes
    d. Improper brake fluid   d. Drain the fluid, remove all rubber parts, and flush the system with proper brake fluid. Install new rubber parts, including check valve and seat

Excessive pressure on pedal, poor stop
    a. Oil on brake shoe lining   a. Replace lining. Locate point of leakage and clean wheel brake
    b. Improper brake shoe lining   b. Replace lining, use genuine spare parts

Brakes tie up while driving
    a. By-pass port in master cylinder not free   a. Clean by-pass port by means of a piece of suitable wire. Remove any burr. Replace cup
        (possibly caused by a deformed cup)
    b. Improper brake fluid   b. Drain the fluid, flush the system and refill with proper brake fluid
    c. Incorrect position of brake pedal stop plate   c. Check position of brake pedal and adjust the pedal play so as to ensure that the by-pass port is not closed by the piston cup

Brakes uneven
    a. Brake drum eccentric   a. Replace brake drum or remachine it
    b. Tires not properly inflated or worn   b. Check tire pressure and replace worn tires
    c. Oil on brake shoe lining   c. Replace lining. Only replace in axle sets (both front wheels or both rear wheels)

Brakes chatter and tend to tie up
    a. Brake shoe lining not chamfered at ends   a. Genuine VW lining is correctly chamfered
    b. Brake shoe lining worn, rivets make contact with the drum   b. Replace lining or reset the rivets
    c. Brake drum eccentric   c. Replace brake drum or remachine it

Brakes noisy
    a. Improper brake shoe lining. Lining not chamfered at ends   a. Reline the shoes. Use Genuine VW Spare Parts
    b. Lining loose on shoe   b. Reline the shoes
    c. Brakes dirty   c. Clean wheel brakes

EXPLANATION OF ENGINE CAPACITY

In Europe or Great Britain the displacement of an engine is usually given in liters (or "litres"), whereas in the United States displacement is generally referred to in terms of cubic inches. Below is table for converting liters to cubic inches:

1/2 liter	30.5125	cu. in.
1	61.025	"
1 1/2	91.5375	"
2	122.050	"
2 1/2	152.5625	"
3	183.073	"
3 1/2	213.5855	"
4	244.100	"
4 1/2	274.6125	"
5	305.125	"
5 1/2	330.6375	"
6	366.150	"
6 1/2	396.6625	"
7	427.175	"

DECIMAL EQUIVALENTS

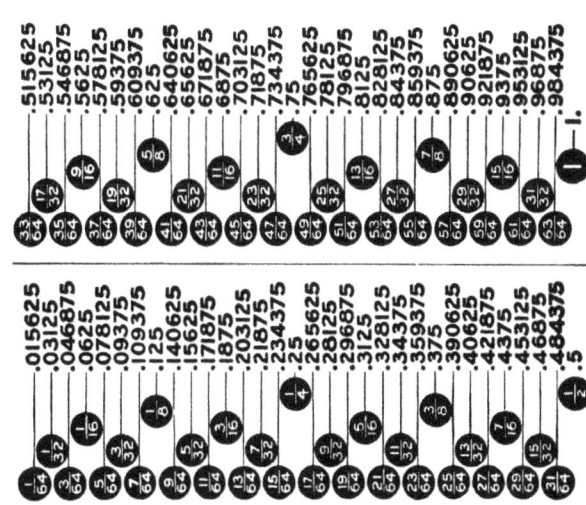

NOTATIONS OF CHANGES
Between 1957, 1958 and 1959 Models

VW MODEL 1957	VW MODEL 1958	VW MODEL 1959
Light metal camshaft gear for all sedans. Formerly: Resitex material	No alteration	No alteration
Oil bath air cleaner now "Knecht" make with toggle-type cover. Formerly: Wing nut	Modified shape (higher, but of smaller outside diameter)	No alteration
Oil cooler, soft soldered	Short design, hard soldered	No alteration
Silencer: Single chamber with 2 exhaust tail pipes. Formerly: 1 tail pipe	No alteration	No alteration
Fuel tank: Cardboard layer between floor and luggage compartment	Fuel tank: Plastic foam layer between floor and luggage compartment	No alteration
Carburetor: Light metal venturi	Carburetor: Plastic venturi	No alteration
Steering wheel: Splined fit 48 teeth Formerly: 24 teeth	No alteration	No alteration
Turning circle approx. 36.1 ft.	Turning circle approx. 36.1 ft	Turning circle approx. 34.4 ft
Accelerator lever provided with a roller	Accelerator pedal provided with a rubber covered pedal	No alteration
Instrument panel: Opening for loudspeaker in the center, ashtray on the right side of loudspeaker.	Instrument panel: Opening for loudspeaker on the left of speedometer, larger pull-out ashtray in the center, glove compartment widened by 50%	No alteration
Side panels partly covered with textile fabric	Side panels completely covered with plastic material	No alteration
Heating channels in lower body members for better heater efficiency. Formerly: Lower body members used as heater channels.	No alteration	No alteration
Synthetic bush with rubber casing for steering column tube	Plastic bush, 50% smaller, spring-loaded laminae	No alteration
Pinion assembly: Roller bearing	Pinion assembly: Needle bearing	No alteration

NOTATIONS OF CHANGES
Between 1957, 1958 and 1959 Models

VW MODEL 1957	VW MODEL 1958	VW MODEL 1959
Rear mainshaft bearing, ball bearing	Rear mainshaft bearing, needle bearing	No alteration
Tubeless tires 5.60 x 15 Formerly: With inner tube	No alteration	No alteration
Brake shoes width 30 mm	Brake shoes width 40 mm	No alteration
Windshieldwiper motor equipped with brake band	Windshieldwiper motor equipped with permanent magnetic brake	No alteration
	Windshieldwiper: Distance between wiper arms reduced, longer blades, larger sweeping area	No alteration
		Fuel pump equipped with a strainer in front of the suction valve
		Plastic packings between rear axle tube retainer and transmission case
	Vision area of windshield enlarged by 17%. The windshield was enlarged towards the top and the sides which resulted in narrower door pillars.	No alteration
	Vision area of the rear view window enlarged by 95%. The window is wider and higher.	No alteration

SPARK PLUGS

If the mixture is correct and the plugs are running at the right temperature, the color of the insulator near the electrodes should be light to darkish brown, depending on the desired mixture strength. If the plug base is wet and sooty, the plug is too cold

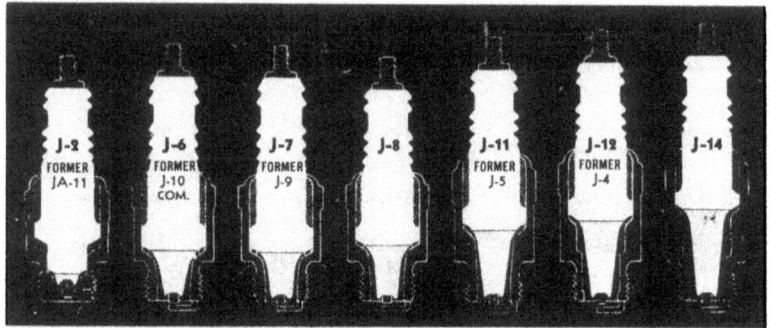

Heat range of Champion spark plugs. The plug on the left is the coldest, the one on the right, the hottest.

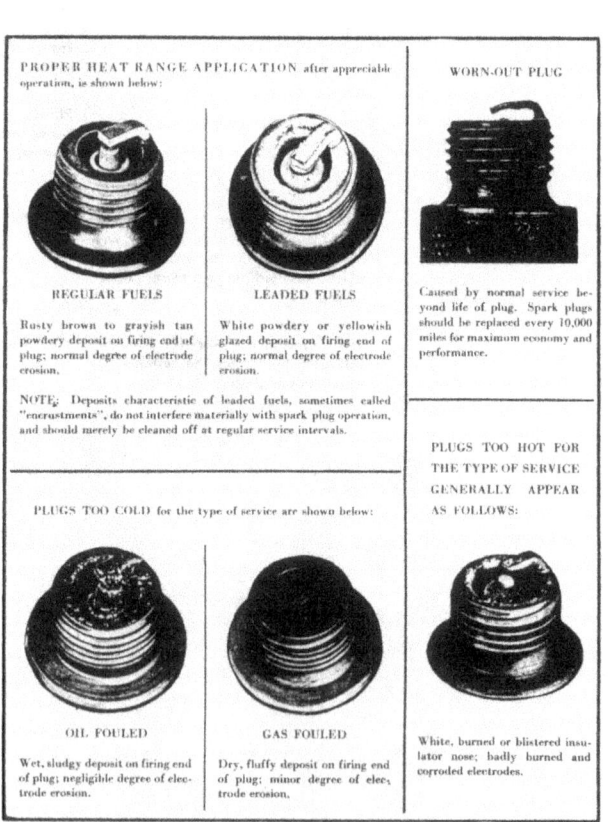

Appearance of the plug indicates what is happening inside the combustion chamber, and whether a colder or hotter plug type should be installed.

HINTS AND TIPS
ON DRIVING A VOLKSWAGEN
By Floyd Clymer

If you are not familiar with a rear engine car you should take it easy with your Volkswagen for your first few trips. You will want to get acquainted with the behavior of the VW, as there is especially some difference in the handling on turns as against driving a front engine car.

Most drivers are inclined to "over steer" a rear engine car. Actually, this presents no problem but requires less turn of the wheel to correct the direction of the car. Always remember that the weight distribution of the VW is probably different from anything you have been accustomed to driving previously. The reason is that in the VW approximately 60% of the weight of the car is in the rear.

In approaching a curve you should not accelerate. However, when you are coming out of a corner or curve you should accelerate for better control of the car. The degree of acceleration depends upon whether the curve is a sharp or a gradual one. It is best not to use the brake on a rear engine car while actually making the turn, and there is some tendency for the rear end to sway especially on wet pavements or on icy or snowy highways or on loose gravel. Therefore, accelerating a rear engine car under any of these conditions will cause the car to skid more quickly than if you are driving a front engine car under the same conditions.

Be sure to familiarize yourself with the controls and the instruments on your new Volkswagen. Actually, there are only a few things that really need your attention, as the operation of the car is extremely simple and you will find no unneeded controls or unnecessary gadgets on your VW. Inside the speedometer there are two warning lights. As soon as the engine starts the warning lights should go off. If they go on while driving, this is an indication that something is wrong and you should stop the car immediately and trace the trouble.

The red warning light indicates that the cooling system is not working properly and, of course, this should be checked. The first thing to look for should the red light go on is to check the fan belt. The fan belt operates both the generator and the cooling fan, and every VW owner should carry a spare fan belt in case of emergency.

The green warning light is your oil control. Always make sure that your crank case is filled. Should the green light go on while you are driving stop the car at once to check your crank case oil level.

On the fire wall directly in front of the gear shift lever is a gasoline tank control lever, and there are three positions in which this lever can be turned. No. 1, vertical position, means that the valve is open; No. 2, horizontal position, means that the reserve tank is on; and No. 3, on an angle between vertical and horizontal,

Three-way fuel tap 1-normal position, 2-reserve, 3-shut off

is the shut-off position. Make sure, whenever you switch to reserve, that the lever is in a 90° angle from the open position — otherwise, it would shut off the fuel supply completely. After the tank has been filled, always remember to put the lever back to position No. 1. (Vertical — you are then running on the main tank.)

Starting the engine — Even in cold weather, the VW engine starts easily and it can be accomplished in two ways. (1) Pull the choke button on the dash out as far as possible and start the engine. In this instance do not touch the accelerator pedal. (2) As you become better acquainted with your Volkswagen, you can easily start the engine without touching the choke, by simply pumping the accelerator pedal up and down a few times. This operation injects a small amount of gasoline into the carburetor throat, thus actually priming the engine. Usually the engine will respond immediately, even in the coldest weather and, by this method, use of the choke is usually unnecessary.

In hot weather, or when the engine is hot or even warm, you should be careful not to pump the accelerator pedal up and down; to do so will cause the warm engine to flood by injecting too much gas in the warm carburetor and manifold.

If your engine is cold you should adjust the idling speed with the choke button, but be sure to push the button back to its normal driving position after the engine temperature becomes normal.

It is always bad to race the engine immediately after starting, especially in cold weather. Air-cooled engines warm up quite easily

— however, they cool off much quicker than water-cooled engines. They are nosier as they have no water jackets to deaden the noise.

When you get on to the knack of shifting gears in your Volkswagen you will find it a fascinating and easy operation. Always remember that only second, third and fourth gears are fully synchronized. First gear is not, and therefore you should not shift into first gear while the car is in motion. First gear should be used only for starting, or for climbing extremely steep hills. Always shift from first to second as quickly as possible.

In order to save the transmission and engine from undue stress, you should shift down from fourth to third between speeds of 47 and 25 mph. Shift from third to second between speeds of 31 and 15 mph. Do not ride the clutch (let your foot rest on the clutch pedal) while standing or at a stop light, as this will cause undue wear on the clutch thrust bearing. Always put the shift level in neutral before starting. Some drivers also like to release the clutch while starting the engine.

To shift into reverse gear, the vehicle must come to a complete stop and there is, of course, a slight resistance requiring some additional effort to get the car into reverse so that this does not happen accidentally.

When driving make sure that your foot rests steadily on the accelerator pedal as this will give you better economy than pumping the throttle or making jack rabbit starts. Quick movement of the throttle up and down only causes higher fuel consumption and flooding in hot weather.

Fortunately there is no breaking-in period required on Volkswagens — you may drive your car with safety as fast as you desire, even when it is new. The recommended speeds for the gears are: (1) 0 to 15 mph; (2) 10 to 30 mph; (3) 25 to 40 mph; (4) 40 to 70 mph. While the VW will considerably exceed 70 mph speeds, the conservative driver will operate his VW at speeds of less than 70 mph.

The VW engine is small in capacity. It gets its best performance by fairly high revolutions and not by "lugging." Be sure to shift down when the engine appears to be under strain. Do not be afraid to "rev up" or "turn over" the engine to secure better acceleration and for climbing hills.

The VW engine, due to its small size, is inclined to be "rough" in operation when it is under stress. U.S. drivers who have long been accustomed to trying to climb certain hills or make long grades in high gear should forget this practice with the VW. On a certain type of grade which the Volkswagen might possibly climb in fourth gear, usually its efficiency would be greatly improved if the car were shifted down to third and the engine allowed to turn over at a higher number of revolutions per minute.

While you should never race the engine, regardless of whether your car is stationary or in motion, always remember that neither should you overwork the engine or stall it driving too slowly in high gear. The VW engine requires a constant flow of air for cooling and this air flow is caused only while running the engine at a fairly fast speed, regardless of what gear the car is in. Overloading, therefore, is harmful to the engine and will cause it to over-heat much faster than the engine turning over at a reasonably high speed.

For all normal operations and driving within speed limits on all highways, no injury can possibly come to the VW engine when in good condition. It is a fantastic car and will take a tremendous amount of abuse, but the owner should realize that it is a different kind of automobile. It is so unconventional in many respects that certain previously-acquired driving habits should be abandoned.

Every new Volkswagen owner should really consider himself a novice until he has driven the car a few hundred miles and has become thoroughly familiar with its behavior and its unconventional design and features.

Other Volkswagen books available from:
www.VelocePress.com
Please visit our website for the most up-to-date information

Volkswagen Beetle 1968-1977

Workshop Manual – Autobooks
Covers 1200, 1300 & 1500 Series and Karmann Ghia

Coming Soon

Volkswagen Transporter

Workshop Manual – Clymer
Covers all Trucks and Vans through 1970

Volkswagen 1500 & 1600

Workshop Manual – Clymer
Covers Station Wagon, Fastback, Notchback & Karmann Ghia through 1970

Volkswagen Beetle 1949-1970

Workshop Manual – Clymer
Covers all models through 1970

All VelocePress titles are available through your local independent bookseller, Amazon.com or direct from VelocePress. Wholesale customers may also purchase direct or from the Ingram book group.

www.ingramcontent.com/pod-product-compliance
Lightning Source LLC
Chambersburg PA
CBHW070600170426
43201CB00012B/1885